Skeleton gig. The author with her part arab stallion Ali. *Photo by J. S. Pearson.*

Alexandra dog cart. Mrs Sanders Watney driving her Welsh cob, Shandy. *Photo by Pony/Light Horse.*

3 Crane Neck Phaeton. *Lent to Science Museum London by Capt. Sir John Lionel Armytage.*

4 The pupil learning to pull a load and to be accustomed to noise. *Photo by Daphne Machin Goodall.*

5 Pony Phaeton. Mrs B. Stewart-Smith driving Whiskey. *Photo by Monty.*

Mail Phaeton. Mr Sanders Watney driving a pair of coach horses (note the perch and platform springs). *Photo by W. S. Pearson.*

Demi Mail Phaeton. Mr Jack Gillam driving a pair of Cleveland Bays. *Photo by C. H. Wood (Bradford) Ltd.*

8 Mr Richard James driving a tandem of hackneys to a gig. *Photo by John Nestle.*

9 Cocking Cart. Mr George Mossman with a tandem (note the tandem bars

Curricle (note curricle bar) driven by Mr George Mossman.
Photo by Monty.

Members of the British Driving Society during a drive through the
New Forest led by Mrs J. Ford. *Photo by Simon N. Rowley.*

12 Ralli Car. Miss Mary Woodcock driving Misty. *Photo by W. S. Pearson.*

13 Four-Wheeled Dog Cart. Mrs E. Parsons with her New Forest ponies, Garth Remus and Deeracres Sally. *Photo by Photonews.*

Country Cart. Mr and Mrs Bryan Thrower with their Welsh Cob
lan Mandarin. *Photo by Peter Le Nevé-Foster, A.R.P.S.*

Governess Car. Mrs Serjeant's Shetland pony, John Willie.
o by Sound Amplification Ltd.

16 Sleigh. The author with Ali. *Photo by Bury Free Press.*

17 Basket Ralli. Miss Ward driving her Dales pony (note Cee springs). *Photo by David Dunn.*

18 The pupil on the long reins. *Photo by Daphne Machin Goodall.*

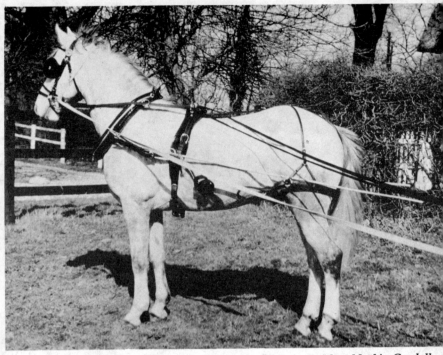

19 The pupil being introduced to shafts. *Photo by Daphne Machin Goodall.*

20 The pupil on the lunge. *Photo by Daphne Machin Goodall.*

A Guide to Driving Horses

SALLIE WALROND

A Guide to Driving Horses

Cover photography by Becky Hance

Mrs. Pam Cannon, assisted by her niece Lori Schultheiss, driving her Morgan, Lookaway's Bo Regard.

Melvin Powers
Wilshire Book Company

12015 Sherman Road, No. Hollywood, CA 91605

THOMAS NELSON AND SONS LIMITED

36 Park Street London W1Y 4DE
PO Box 18123 Nairobi Kenya

THOMAS NELSON (AUSTRALIA) LTD
597 Little Collins Street Melbourne 3000

THOMAS NELSON AND SONS (CANADA) LTD
81 Curlew Drive Don Mills Ontario

THOMAS NELSON (NIGERIA) LTD
PO Box 336 Apapa Lagos

THOMAS NELSON AND SONS (SOUTH AFRICA)
(Proprietary) Ltd 51 Commissioner Street Johannesburg

This book first published 1971
© Sallie Walrond 1971
PRINTED IN THE UNITED STATES OF AMERICA

ISBN 0-87980-242-1

CONTENTS

ACKNOWLEDGEMENTS

The author would like to thank Mr and Mrs Sanders Watney and Mr Jack Gillam for their generous help and advice and for permission to reproduce photographs; Mr E. E. Burroughes, Mrs J. D. Greene and Miss Cordelia Hislop for their kind assistance; Miss P. Nuttall-Smith for permission to reproduce Figure 43; and Mrs J. Ford, Mr Richard James, Mr George Mossman, Mrs E. Parsons, Mrs R. B. Serjeant, Mrs B. Stewart-Smith, Mr and Mrs B. Thrower, Miss J. Ward, Miss Mary Woodcock, David Dunn, Peter Le Neve-Foster, A.R.P.S., Daphne Machin Goodall, Lt. Col. C. E. G. Hope, Monty, John Nestle, W. S. Pearson, Simon N. Rowley, The Science Museum, Sound Amplification Ltd, Frederick E. Spicer, West Suffolk Newspapers Ltd, and C. H. Wood (Bradford) Ltd, for permission to reproduce photographs.

ILLUSTRATIONS

(between pages 56 and 57)

Chapter 1

A BRIEF HISTORY OF DRIVING IN ENGLAND

The first horse-drawn vehicles in England were the sledge-like contraptions invented by the Ancient Britons. When the horse first became domesticated loads were fixed to its back. Then someone discovered that a larger burden could be transported if it was tied behind the horse. A pair of poles was fixed to the horse by means of a neckstrap and surcingle and the ends were left to drag along the ground, the load being tied across them. Ancient Britons' sledges probably ran quite well over grassy and icy surfaces and would have dragged through the mud rather better than any wheeled vehicle.

Chariots, with two wheels and a pole, as used by Queen Boadicea, were driven with a pair or with three or four horses harnessed abreast. These vehicles were used for fighting and racing. It is not thought that they were ever employed for the purpose of carrying passengers or luggage.

The magnificent roads built by the Romans rapidly deteriorated after their makers' departure from England and travel by vehicle thereafter was such a slow and exhausting business that it was easier to ride on a horse than behind one. The difficulty involved in hauling a wheeled vehicle virtually across country through quagmires in winter and deep ruts in summer must have been a tremendous and impracticable exercise.

1

Agricultural carts, however, were in use about 1,000 years ago pulled by oxen and horses, but these were not suitable conveyances for passengers. The roads were so bad in the country that during the winter months or in a wet summer it became impossible for animals to drag a heavily laden waggon to its destination. Because of the absence of roads, use was made of streams and shallow rivers, the stony bottoms of which afforded a far better surface for pulling a wheeled load than the alternative choice of a route across a field. These streams became converted over the course of years, into ready-made roads and the water from them diverted to run

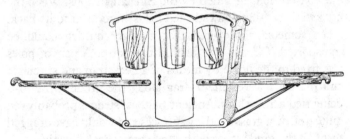

Fig. 1 A litter

alongside. It is interesting to note, particularly in East Anglia, the number of lanes which now run alongside streams and which, in all probability, began in this way.

The horse litter (Fig. 1) was a method devised to transport a passenger who was unable to ride. The litter was a carrying couch with poles fore and aft into which two horses were harnessed. This method avoided the use of wheels and was advantageous for conveying the sick or aged. Litters were used to some extent for state purposes, and on those occasions were furnished with elaborate materials for the benefit of the ladies of high rank who rode in them: the horses too, were adorned with magnificent trappings. It is recorded that

Catherine of Aragon, in 1509, rode in a litter and was accompanied by ladies in covered chariots. One presumes therefore, that the litter was considered a superior conveyance to the available four-wheeled chariots which were not much more than unsprung boxes on wheels.

Nonetheless, by 1553 the four-wheeled chariot had advanced in status. Queen Mary Tudor, accompanied by Princess Elizabeth and Ann of Cleves, rode in one drawn by six horses, to her coronation. Fifty years before she would have ridden in a litter, so there must have been considerable improvements in chariot building during that time.

It is believed that the first introduction of a coach into England was one which was built for the Earl of Rutland by Walter Rippon in 1555, and within twenty-five years coaches were in general use amongst the rich members of the community. Matters came to such a state that by the beginning of the seventeenth century there was considerable concern regarding the excessive use of coaches. It was feared that they would encourage idleness and effeminacy in men and that the standard of British horsemanship would deteriorate. In 1601 a Bill to curb the use of coaches was read, but rejected, in Parliament. Coaches at this period of course, were still restricted to London and other large towns where there were passable road surfaces available for their use.

During this time the stage-, long-, or flying-waggon was in use. This was a very heavy and cumbersome vehicle operating solely for the purpose of carrying people and goods from the larger country towns to London. It was hauled by teams of six, eight or ten heavy horses which were driven by a waggoner either on foot or mounted. Travel with such an equipage must have been extremely wearying, since the average speeds were probably not more than three miles an hour. The name flying-waggon was given to this mode of

3

transport because it was considered such an improvement on the pack horse! As the number of these waggons increased they began to be built with wheels resembling road rollers. The idea was that these would flatten and improve the rough roads and would prevent the waggons themselves from becoming bogged. In fact, they made the roads worse, because during wet weather the rollers dug huge channels, making deep ruts for following traffic to negotiate.

The London taxi cab, as it is now known, appeared in the form of a four-wheeled hackney coach in the early seventeenth century, the word hackney coming from the French word *haquenée*, meaning a horse for hire. The appearance of this vehicle caused anger and dismay amongst the Thames watermen, who, up to that time, had had sole monopoly of passenger traffic in London. Frequently, these early hackney coaches were vehicles which had been discarded from private service. When the wheels of the family coach had become damaged and the body shaken, rich owners disposed of their vehicle, and many a once-dashing coach finished its days in the hands of the hackney proprietor.

These coaches were originally based at the coach proprietor's yard whence they were hired. By 1634, a stand for hackney coaches were established in the Strand, and at the same time Sedan chairs were introduced. This further innovation brought even more jealousy, as the watermen, seeing their trade diminishing, resented these chairmen just as much as the hackney coachmen. The coaches, however, caused such traffic jams in the narrow streets of London that in 1635 Charles I forbade their use in the City unless the passenger was making a journey of three miles or more out of London. This royal decree successfully reduced the number of coaches for a few years.

The first stage coaches, which were heavy and virtually

unsprung vehicles, only started in about 1640 and the roads, even then, were so bad that the coaches could only be used during the summer months. Contemporary writers report that these coaches were exceedingly uncomfortable to ride in and they were very slow. In 1658, for instance, it took four days to journey from Exeter to London in one of these cumbersome vehicles.

Some twenty-five years after the action of Charles I against the hackney coaches of London the number of vehicles had increased again; this time to a point where they were considered to constitute a public nuisance. As a result they were forbidden to stand in the streets or to ply for hire, and had to remain in yards until they were required. Finally, in an effort to improve conditions for travellers, a law was passed by Charles II which led to a drastic reduction in the number of hackney coaches. Commissioners were appointed and charged with the issue of just four hundred licences. No hackney coach was permitted to operate without one and, not surprisingly, this led to much bribery, and many of the unfortunates who could not obtain licences set up in towns within twenty miles of London, whence they drove up to the city each day and often plied at night in order to escape discovery.

By 1663 a cumbersome type of coach, sometimes pulled by a postillion-driven pair, was being used, and prints of the period show uncovered boxes protruding from either side of these bulky vehicles. Two unfortunate travellers, usually of low rank, sat in the doorways with their legs and feet in these boxes, which were known as 'boots', and this is the origin of the term. The fare from Lancashire to London in one of these vehicles was 30s. – a large sum in comparison with today's money values.

The same year saw the first turnpike gate on the Great

5

North Road which collected tolls for the roads leading to Cambridge, Hertfordshire and Huntingdonshire. This was an excellent development, although most unpopular, and one which led eventually, to vastly improved roads throughout England. Better roads brought about advances in the coach building trade and encouraged the breeding of lighter, faster horses. As vehicles became grander more and more horses were harnessed together. No doubt the frightful country roads made it necessary to use a six-horse team for hauling the coach through the mud and ruts, but in London as many as eight horses were put to, just for show, each enthusiast trying to outdo his neighbour.

After the Great Fire of London in 1666 the streets of the capital were widened and improved and the passage of traffic was accordingly made easier. A little under thirty years later the licences available for hackney coaches were increased to 700 and provided a little of the much-needed revenue required to pursue the war with France. A charge of £50 was made for a licence having a life of twenty-one years, and on top of this the proprietors had an annual rent of £4 to find.

By 1706 coaching had progressed so quickly, owing to the improvements in the roads made possible by the turnpike system, that a London-to-York coach left on Mondays, Wednesdays and Fridays and took only four days to complete the 200-mile journey. Passengers were allowed 14 lb of luggage with threepence per pound payable for excess baggage, but the hazards of such a journey were still very considerable. In 1736, for instance, there was reported to be an impassable gulf of mud between Kensington and London. Although some lengths of road were reasonably good, it was quite usual to get stuck on the less good stretches, and delays, whilst extra horses were brought up to help coach teams, were commonplace. Coach design had made certain progress but

6

coaches, in the main, were top-heavy, particularly when loaded, and very susceptible to overturning. As an additional worry there was the highwayman, for whom the lumbering coaches provided good and relatively easy pickings. Travellers certainly needed a strong constitution to submit themselves to the rigours of such journeys and it is not surprising that wills were often written and prayers said before venturing forth.

Outside passengers on these coaches were perched precariously on the top with nothing to hold on to and if one of them happened to go to sleep he chanced dropping off. Hence the modern cliche 'to drop off'.

The coaches had accommodation for eight inside and a large open-topped basket over the rear axle was used for carrying some of the outside passengers. Straw was put in the basket in cold weather to give a little warmth to the unfortunate occupants, who, if the coach was crowded, had to stand for the duration of their journey. Later, an open wooden box replaced the basket, and then a lid was put on and the passengers sat on the top. This box became known as the hind boot.

In 1768 three gold medals were awarded to Dr R. Lovell Edgeworth by the Society of English Arts and Manufacturers for inventing a method of springing. A number of types of spring were being tried out at the time in order to relieve both horses and passengers of the discomfort which they had suffered in the past. Private coaches had become lighter by this date and whip springs (Fig. 2) were in more general use. This slight springing caused vehicles to run more easily and led to the erroneous belief that the higher a coach was loaded the better its progress. The height of public coaches was considerable and they frequently were overladen with both passengers and luggage to a dangerous degree. One story tells of a vehicle carrying thirty-four passengers plus baggage which got away with no more than a broken brace, but there were many more serious accidents due to overloading and bad design.

By the end of the eighteenth century, the increase in road coaches and the number of accidents in which they were involved made it necessary for legislation to be introduced lowering the height of vehicles and limiting the number of passengers which might be carried.

The mail had been carried for years by mounted post-boys,

Fig. 2 Whip spring

but in 1784 the first mail coach drawn by four horses appeared, and by 1799 there were eighty mail coaches leaving London each day, the mail being taken from the London GPO to the various departure points by gig.

The extension of the mail service resulted in the creation of a new official, the mail guard, who travelled on the coach. He had to be a robust person and of the highest character. Indeed, he could only be appointed on the recommendation of an M.P. As well as being responsible for the safe delivery of the mail and passengers, he was in charge of the well-being and punctuality of the coach. He had to have a sound knowledge of running repairs to coach and harness and if the vehicle got stuck in a snow drift, or otherwise delayed, it was his lot to get help or alternatively to ride one of the horses and deliver the mail, mounted. He sat in solitary confinement over the boot of the coach with a cocked blunderbuss to ward off potential robbers, and for all this he received about 10s. a week plus perquisites earned by taking special care of valuables and by receiving a percentage of short-journey passenger fares.

A tremendous class snobbery existed between the outside passengers on a coach and those travelling inside. So much so that if a passenger riding outside wished to change to an inside seat during the journey it could only be done at the request of an inside passenger, who then had to have that outside passenger sitting next to him.

The famous 'Golden Age of Coaching,' which only lasted from 1815 to about 1840, was largely due to two men, John Macadam, the road builder, who perfected the process known as 'macadamising', and Telford, the engineer.

Improved roads naturally produced faster coaches and none was considered better than the Royal Mail, which was accordingly more expensive than the ordinary run of road coaches. Such was the punctuality of the mail coach that villagers set their timepieces by its daily passing. Turnpike gates were opened in anticipation at the sound of the guard's approaching horn, since the mail was exempt from tolls and every second was important if the schedule was to be kept. Changing horses became a fine art and was accomplished in seconds rather than minutes, and the mail was helped further in maintaining its reputation for punctuality by having right of way over all other traffic.

Faster roads led also to reckless coachmanship, and amongst the less well-run coaches accidents occurred through drunken driving, wheels breaking and coaches being overturned. Coaching, not surprisingly, developed a language of its own: 'feather edging it' was driving too close to something; the whip was known as 'the tool'; 'springing them' was the term used for galloping. The road coach team frequently worked 'two sweats', the same team working twice on the same day; once on each side of the road, that is, on the outward journey and again on the return trip. It was quite usual to divide a journey into three 'grounds' of ten to fifteen miles each, the first being known as the 'upper ground', the last the 'lower ground', near the towns and then the 'middle ground' where doubtful horses were sometimes used. On this stretch, the poor coachman and luckless passengers might have to put up with the whims of a team consisting of three bolters and a blind one. Diseased and sick horses were often kept for night runs where their disorders probably passed unnoticed, a malpractice which unfortunately led to the spread of infection to sound animals. The estimated average working life of a coach horse on a fast run was about four years.

Meanwhile, a large number of private coaches were being used by the wealthy. Some were owner-driven and others were coachman-driven. Although expensive, the convenience of private ownership overcame the disadvantages of stage and mail coach travel.

By the end of the eighteenth century vehicles were being built to customers' specifications in every conceivable shape and size to satisfy individual whims all over the country. Perhaps the most famous of the coach builders of the time was William Felton, who was responsible for designing many beautiful carriages which later came into everyday employment. The word carriage now generally used for the whole vehicle should, strictly speaking, refer to that part which is now known as the under carriage.

The turn of the century found cee springs (Fig. 3) taking

the place of whip springs, and these added considerably to the comfort of vehicles.

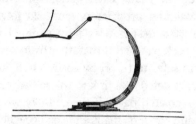

Fig. 3 Cee spring

The elliptic spring (Fig. 4) was used in 1805 by a coach builder named Elliot and was probably the greatest single improvement in carriage design. Up to this time, the perch had been an essential part of the vehicle, but by using the new spring the perch was no longer an integral part and a far greater freedom was open to designers.

Fig. 4 Elliptic spring

Driving, largely through the influence of the Prince of Wales, had quickly been taken up as a sport by the 'bloods' of the time and driving clubs were formed in 1807 and 1808. These were the Benson Driving Club and the Four Horse Club, respectively. The former lasted for fifty years and the latter had an active life for eighteen years.

A three-horse public omnibus, the forerunner of our present bus system, was introduced in 1829. It carried twenty-two passengers and provided a library to relieve boredom during travel.

By the 1830s, when coaching had reached the height of its efficiency, the new railways were offering strong competition and the decline of the road coach became inevitable. To begin with, the coaching proprietors tendered lower fares. Hopefully, or perhaps desperately, they claimed that the view from a road coach was better than that from a rail coach and also that it was safer to travel by road. Then, accepting the situation, coaches acted as a link to the railways. Finally, coaches just ran to isolated parts of the country where there were no railways, and carriers, mails and road coaches gradually disappeared from the roads. Private and coachman-driven carriages continued for many years after 1830, frequently being carried during part of their long journeys on a train. In addition, driving continued to flourish as a sport and even in 1850 on-the-spot fines for furious driving were frequent. The Four in Hand Driving Club was formed in 1856 and the still-flourishing Coaching Club in 1870.

It was estimated in 1891 that there were 300,000 horses working in and around London in various capacities such as coal haulage, fire fighting and funeral work, and a tremendous number of horses were still being driven for pleasure. One report states that on an Epsom Derby day in 1892, 4,002 horses passed along the road by Clapham Common between 5 p.m. and 9 p.m., on their way home from the races.

Gradually, the working horses were replaced by the internal combustion engines and, tragically, many vehicles deemed unwanted were broken up and burned. Spokes were used as ladder staves. Between the wars enthusiasts still drove their horses for pleasure and a revival, albeit born of necessity, occurred during World War II when petrol rationing caused vehicles to be unearthed and horses put to harness work once again.

The year 1957 saw the birth of the British Driving Society,

which was founded by a group of dedicated enthusiasts led by Mr Sanders Watney. The inaugural meeting was held at the Royal Windsor Horse Show in 1958 when about forty turn-outs were present. Since then, infected by Mr Watney's enthusiasm, the Society has enrolled over 1,000 members. Vehicles have been found and restored, horses broken and put to and the art of harness-making has been revived. Most large shows and a number of smaller fixtures hold driving classes and non-competitive meets, rallies and drives are organised by the Society's Area Commissioners throughout the British Isles.

It is encouraging to think that, in spite of the advent of the English steam carriage, the coming of the railways and the invention of the internal combustion engine, the sport of driving has survived.

Chapter 2

SINGLE HORSE

The newcomer to private driving will probably start his career with second-hand harness, but great care should be taken when purchasing such a set since harness found in sales may be of dubious condition and quality. Leather on which only boot polish has been used can look magnificent at first glance but is probably dry and brittle underneath through lack of oiling. When leather is bent it should not show tiny cracks; if it does it may well snap as soon as any sudden strain is applied.

In a few cases, plastic is now being used for harness, but, although this may look all right on winkers, it is not to be recommended for surfaces such as the lining of the pad, as plastic cannot readily absorb sweat. Nor should it be used for those parts which bear strain.

It is probably best, if it is at all possible, to buy privately from someone who has looked after the leather properly, keeping it soft and supple on the inside and polished on the outside surfaces. Having purchased a set, check every strap and buckle. If in doubt about any part – renew it.

The parts of single horse harness are shown in Fig. 5.

Harnessing. When harnessing the horse the collar is put on first. Before placing it over the animal's head it is advisable to stretch it by putting one's knee against the lining and pulling upwards. This temporarily widens the collar. A horse can quickly become shy of having his collar put on if it is forced against the sensitive skin above his eyes, and for this reason the collar goes on upside down, to enable its widest part to pass over the broadest point of the head. It is left like this

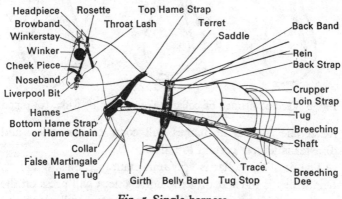

Fig. 5 Single harness

whilst the hames (with their traces attached and coiled around themselves in a figure-of-eight loop), are placed into position in the groove of the collar. The top hame strap, which is now at the bottom, is done up tightly enough to hold the hames in place whilst the collar is turned round. The collar should be turned at the narrowest part of the horse's throat, going with the direction of the mane and then pushed down into position against the shoulders. The top hame strap is now tightened so that the hames are held firmly into their groove in the collar. The hames are secured at the bottom by another hame strap or hame chain. If the latter is used, it should be made of steel, plated with brass if the hames are brass plated, so that both match. Manganese bronze, a modern alloy which is similar to brass in appearance, is also satisfactory for use in this connection. Solid brass hame chains are not safe owing to their tendency to break without warning. Great attention should be paid to the hame straps,

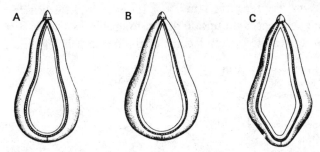

Fig. 6 Various fittings of collar: (a) narrow, (b) wide, (c) piped

for if one breaks the hames will come off the collar and disaster is almost certain to follow.

The fit of the collar is very important (see Figs. 6 and 7). One which is too short for the horse's neck will press on the windpipe whilst a collar which is too narrow will pinch and blister. A wide collar will rock from side to side causing sore shoulders and too long a collar will ride upwards as soon as

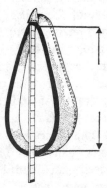

Fig. 7 How to measure a collar

the horse is in draught. A well-fitting collar should lie comfortably and flat on the shoulders with enough room at the bottom to allow the hand to pass freely between it and the horse's neck. It should, however, be remembered that a collar that fits perfectly throughout one summer is very often found to be too small the following year when the horse has developed more muscles on his neck and shoulders.

If a false martingale is used it should be buckled round the hames and the collar so that it holds the bottom of the collar down and keeps the hames in position momentarily if a hame strap should break. (See Fig. 14.)

To avoid the problems inherent in fitting a collar of this type a breast collar can be used. This is far easier to fit but is not considered as smart for showing purposes. A breast collar is not suitable for pulling heavy loads because the weight of the vehicle is localized rather than distributed over the whole of the shoulder area. It consists of a broad, padded strap which passes round the front of the chest, being held up by a narrower strap lying over the neck in front of the withers. Care should be taken that the breast strap is fitted above the points of the shoulders; one which lies too low will chafe very quickly.

The saddle, back band, tugs, belly band, girth, crupper, loin strap, breeching and breeching straps are put on next, in one unit. The saddle is placed in the middle of the horse's back; the breeching is put in its position over the quarters, so that it lies about 12 inches below the dock and rests against the buttocks, and then the crupper is put on. Standing on the nearside of the quarters, the tail is raised and folded in half with the right hand; the tailpiece of the crupper is then placed over the folded tail and eased up into a comfortable position at the top of the dock, making certain that no hairs are caught up. Some cruppers have buckles on the tailpiece and when this is the case, the nearside buckle can be undone, the tail lifted and the crupper put underneath and rebuckled. This is a useful arrangement with a horse who resists the crupper by stiffening his dock. Care should be taken that the dock part of the crupper is kept pliable and that it is wide enough for the horse concerned. A narrow or hard crupper will rapidly chafe the dock and may lead to kicking. Cruppers are usually filled with linseed when they are made to keep them soft, but they still need a great deal of oiling.

The saddle can now be lifted forward and placed well back from the withers in much the same position as a roller would lie. It is a common mistake to put the saddle too far forward, and this can lead to sore elbows and girth galls.

Like the collar, the saddle should fit the horse. A saddle with a broad tree will bear down on the spine of a narrow animal, and conversely a narrow tree will soon pinch a horse with a broad or flat back.

The back strap of the crupper must be fitted tight enough to prevent the pad from slipping forward, but not so tight that continual pressure is put on to the tail.

The girth is done up next, incorporating the false martingale if one is used. The belly band can be left undone as it is easier to put to if the tugs are manoeuvrable. However, if the horse is to be led some considerable distance to his vehicle, the belly band must be buckled or wound round itself to prevent the belly band buckle from getting between the fore legs and swinging about, irritating and possibly bruising the horse as he walks.

The reins are now put on by being threaded through the pad terrets and through the hame terrets. They are then left ready to buckle on to the bridle, the driving end being folded double and tucked either through the offside terret or under the backpiece of the crupper.

The bridle is put on next with the same attention to fitting that would be paid to a riding bridle. The browband must be long enough to ensure that the headpiece and rosettes are not being pulled forward on to the base of the ears. Winkers should be adjusted for height and width by means of the top buckles on the cheek pieces and the centre buckle of the headpiece and winker stays so that their widest part coincides with the point of the eye. Attention to this detail is often neglected and can cause unnecessary discomfort. Winkers which are fitted too low will chafe the tops of the eyes and permit the horse to see out over the top of them. The purpose of winkers is to prevent the horse from becoming frightened by movements of the whip or passengers; in addition a great many horses, even normally calm ones, become unbelievably afraid should they be allowed to see rotating wheels. The top part of the wheels travels forward at twice the speed of the whole vehicle and to the horse, who sees them out of the corner of his eye, this can seem as though the wheels are chasing or indeed overhauling him. The height of the bit is adjusted by the lowermost buckles on the cheek pieces. Care should be taken to see that when pressure is put on to the bit the cheek pieces do not bulge out, which would allow the horse to see behind him. The throatlatch should be tight enough to allow freedom of the throat when the horse flexes. The noseband must be long enough at the front to let the cheek pieces hang straight and done up loose enough at the back to admit two fingers. If a horse pulls by opening his mouth, the noseband can be tightened to prevent this habit.

Last of all, the reins are buckled to the bit.

Choice of Bits. The traditional driving bits for a single horse are the Wilson snaffle (Fig. 8) and the Liverpool bit (Fig. 9). For showing purposes, the latter is considered preferable. If a Wilson snaffle is used the cheek pieces of the bridle are buckled to the floating rings and the reins to both rings. Very severe action can be obtained if the reins are

Fig. 8 Wilson snaffle

buckled to the outside bit rings only as this produces a more violent nutcracker action on the tongue and considerable pressure against the sides of the jaw. Some Liverpool bits

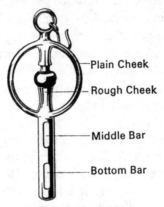

Plain Cheek

Rough Cheek

Middle Bar

Bottom Bar

Fig. 9 Liverpool bit

have up to five possible positions for buckling the reins. Often, one side of the mouth piece is smooth and the other rough so that the whole bit may be reversed to vary its severity. The positions for the reins are: (1) Plain cheek, which gives the equivalent of rough or smooth straight bar snaffle, depending on which side of the bit is put against the tongue. (2) Rough cheek, giving a very mild curb action. (3) Upper bar, which gives slight curb action. (4) Middle bar, putting more severe tension on the curb chain. (5) Lower bar, which can be an extremely strong curb bit. Most Liverpool bits only have two bar fittings on the cheeks, which are known as middle bar and bottom bar. The longer the cheeks of the bit the more leverage there will be on the curb chain when the rein is buckled on the bottom bar.

Some light-mouthed horses will go more kindly if a piece of bicycle inner tubing or chamois leather is wrapped round the mouth piece of the bit and sewn on. Curb chains made from leather or elastic are sometimes more effective than the conventional metal link. Bitting is, of course, extremely important and a horse who is comfortable in his mouth will be far more pleasant to drive than one who continuously fusses with his head.

Care must be taken when leading a harnessed horse from the stable to see that he does not catch the tugs or breeching against the door post or bang his hip. If he does it can encourage him to rush, and knocks received from door posts can result in a dropped hip. It is best to face him square to the doorway and to lead him out slowly by the noseband.

When putting to, the horse should stand still whilst the vehicle is drawn up towards him with the shafts raised well above his quarters. If the horse is young or disobedient and no assistant is available, it is a help to have him facing a wall, which will prevent him from walking off. Backing the horse into the vehicle is a bad practice. When the vehicle is brought up the shafts are put through the tugs until they, the tugs, rest against the tug stop; the traces can then be uncoiled and hooked on to the trace hooks. This should always be done first so that if the horse steps forward the vehicle will go with him and there will not be an accident. If the breeching straps are fastened before the traces the horse is well able to get half-way out of the vehicle and the shafts will probably fall from the tugs, causing both disaster and damage. Any slight difficulty in getting the traces to reach to their hooks can be overcome by pulling the vehicle forward a couple of inches by the step support. This is far preferable to pulling at the trace and asking the horse to step back. Care should be taken to see that the traces are not twisted. Trace hooks on a spring, or swingle tree attachments, are better than the solidly attached trace hooks since, as they give with the movement, they are less likely to cause sore shoulders. The breeching is fastened next. The breeching straps pass round the shafts and traces before being buckled through the forwardmost dees on the shafts. They should be of such a length as to ensure that when the vehicle is pushed forward about four inches, the breeching comes into action against the quarters; the back band will then hang a little in front of the perpendicular and the traces in a slight loop when the breeching is in action. If the breeching is too loose the horse will take all the weight of the vehicle on his back band. When this occurs the tug stops will push against the tugs and the back band will move forward putting tremendous pressure on to the pad and crupper. The pad may then be pushed towards the withers, causing galling at that point and sore elbows.

If false breeching (also known as Brown's patent breeching) is used (Fig. 10) this should be buckled on to the vehicle using the rearmost breeching dees (these are situated about 15 inches from the dashboard) before the horse is brought from the stable. A false breeching consists of a broad padded strap fastened across the width of the shafts by two figure-of-eight shaped metal fittings and two small straps and buckles. These attachments pass through the breeching dees and go round the traces and shafts, holding the breeching in position.

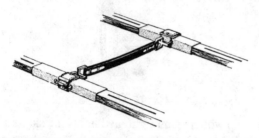

Fig. 10 False breeching, also known as Brown's Patent Breeching

The belly band is passed over the traces and done up last. This is not buckled as tightly as the girth. There should be enough play to enable the shafts of a two-wheeled vehicle to ride up and down slightly. If a four-wheeled vehicle is used, French Tilbury tugs (Fig. 11) will be necessary. These differ

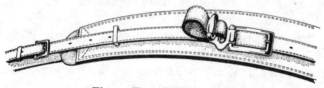

Fig. 11 French Tilbury tug

from ordinary tugs (Fig. 12) in that they hold the shafts rigidly to the pad. They consist of a large buckle which is fastened to a back band and a leather-covered metal half-loop on which the shafts rest. There is a leather strap sewn on to the outside of the loop which passes over the shaft through a slot on the large buckle and through a keeper which is fixed on to the base of the pad. A short belly band is then buckled

Fig. 12 Open tug

to this strap which when tightened holds the shafts still. This belly band should be tighter than an ordinary belly band but not as tight as a girth.

The Whip. The person who drives a horse is known as the Whip. The name originated because of the extreme skill required of a coachman driving a team to apply the whip to a desired animal, the near leader in particular, without hitting or frightening the other three horses or removing his passengers' headwear.

Before mounting the vehicle it is advisable for the Whip to walk round the turn-out and check that all is to his liking. Passengers should not mount until the Whip is safely seated and in full control of his horse from the box seat. The Whip takes the reins in the right hand from their position in the offside terret and stands alongside the offside step of the vehicle with the nearside rein placed under the index finger and the offside rein under the middle finger. This leaves the thumb and index finger free to hold the rail when mounting. The offside rein should be pulled out about 3 inches longer than the nearside rein to ensure that if the horse should step forward during mounting a feel on the reins will keep him straight. Mounting should be carried out quickly and quietly and the Whip should sit down immediately, transferring the reins to the left hand.

The Reins. The nearside rein lies over the index finger and the offside rein goes under the middle finger (Fig. 13).

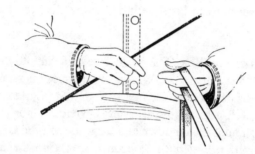

Fig. 13 Holding reins and whip for single or pair driving

Having two fingers between the reins enables pressure to be applied to either rein by rounding the wrist upwards or downwards. The thumb should point to the right and never upwards or press on the rein unless a loop has been taken (see Fig. 30 in Chapter Four). The fore finger should point outwards and slightly to the rear. The middle, third and little fingers press on the reins as they come through the hand, gripping them against the palm to prevent them from slipping. The reins must never be separated and must always stay together in the left hand. The wrist should be kept well rounded, light and supple. It is held about 3 inches in front of the centre of the body with the arm in an horizontal position across the body. A stiff, unyielding, left wrist will probably result in a pulling horse whilst a sympathetic hand with sensitive fingers will often make the hardest puller go kindly. The reins must be held exactly level, and this can be checked by noting whether or not the stitching, where the lengths of rein are joined, are alongside each other. (A pair of single horse reins is cut with four strips of hide and, therefore, has to be joined to give the required length.) If one rein is always held a little tighter than the other the horse will either become onesided in his mouth or go with his head turned a little.

Position on the Box. The elbows are held close to the sides and near to the hips. The Whip should appear as an upright workmanlike figure on the box seat and sit high enough to allow himself a good forward view beyond his horses' ears. His legs should stretch down and forward with the knees and ankles together and the feet planted firmly on the floor or footrest. It is very dangerous to drive without adequate purchase for the feet. If a horse starts to pull or suddenly pecks or falls the Whip could easily be hauled from his precarious perch and will be powerless to assist the horse. Some vehicles have a moveable footrest for the Whip, and when this is so its position should be checked on mounting the vehicle. Too low a box seat is unsatisfactory; nothing looks worse than a Whip sitting on a low seat with knees bent at an acute angle and feet spread apart and, in addition, such a position will prove inadequate if a crisis should arise.

Anyone who has suffered the experience of sitting next to a Whip driving from a low box seat, with a rein in each hand at the end of tense, outstretched arms, whip in socket, will know the sensation of impending catastrophe which is inspired – the horse, as well as the passenger, is filled with a feeling of apprehension.

Using the Whip. As soon as the reins are settled in the left hand and the foot rest is adjusted the whip is taken in the right hand. It is held at the point of balance, usually just beyond the top ferrule, and carried so that it lies lightly and easily under the thumb muscle. The stick part is held at an angle of about 45 degrees across the body with the thong hanging down. The right hand should be held alongside the left with the arm horizontal but is moved rather more than the left in using the whip and assisting on the reins. The whip must always be held when driving and no attempt should ever be made to drive without one. The whip takes the place of a riders' legs, and is used to keep the horse up to his bit and correct him if necessary. When the whip is applied it is laid between the collar and pad or just behind the pad. It should not be used on the quarters as this could lead to kicking. The whip is also used for giving signals. When a turn to the right is intended, it is held horizontally to the right and the thong is swung anti-clockwise. A left-hand turn is signalled by holding it to the left and swinging the thong clockwise. Before stopping, the whip is held upright in front of the centre of the body. When driving alone on public roads, it is probably safest to give car hand signals, with the right hand whilst holding the whip and reins in the left. In the show ring, the occupants of the Royal Box should be saluted on the first circuit of the ring and on the last time round before leaving. The procedure for a lady Whip is to turn her head slightly, give a small bow and raise the whip to an horizontal position. Any female passengers should bow. A gentleman Whip should take his reins and whip in the left hand, turn his head slightly and raise his hat with his right hand. Male passengers should raise their hats. A groom wearing livery should neither turn his head nor remove his hat. If the occasion is very formal, the grooms should remove their hats, placing them on their knees. They should also do this if the coachman is addressed by royalty.

Care of the whip is important, and it is essential that it be kept hanging on a whip reel when it is not in use. The thong lies in the groove on the reel which keeps it in an agreeable shepherd's crook shape. A whip shaped like this is more pleasant to use as the thong swings easily across the horse. If the whip is kept standing in a corner, the stick, which is often made of holly, will rapidly warp.

Moving Off. Having taken up the reins and whip, the apron or knee rug must be adjusted. The passengers may now mount. Once they are safely seated, and have arranged their rugs, the horse may be given the warning that he is going to be asked to move off. Feel his mouth gently before asking him to walk on. If he does not respond to the first request, ask him again before drawing the whip gently across his shoulders. Never slap him on the loins with the reins. There is a tendency for beginners who are more accustomed to riding to sit on the edge of the box seat and wave their hands and legs backwards and forwards in an effort to make a sticky horse go on. The body and legs must be kept still and the hands very light but with a constant contact on the horse's mouth. During the transition from halt to walk it is essential to give slightly with the hand without dropping the feel on the horse's mouth.

A light-mouthed horse met by a dread unsympathetic hand will probably throw up his head and stop. The next time that he is asked he will hesitate and then, plucking up courage, will plunge forward into his collar. This is a bad habit which is easily formed and hard to cure. When he is asked to go on, the horse should lower his head and neck, lean into his collar and walk forward boldly without any jerking. Once a horse starts hesitating to go forward because of heavy hands, he may become really nappy and jib.

Vehicle Balance. A horse should be driven for the first half-mile or so at the walk, to give him time to settle. Whilst he is doing so the Whip can check that all the harness is fitted correctly and that the vehicle, if it is a two-wheeler, is balancing properly. When the animal is in draught the backband should lie on the pad in a perpendicular line. If, when the traces are taut, the backband hangs behind the perpendicular, off the pad, or if the tugs are lying too far in front of the tug stops instead of against them, then the traces are too long and should be taken up a hole or two. The breeching should hang about 4 inches behind the quarters when the horse and vehicle are going on a level surface.

The vehicle should balance so that the shafts lie lightly in the tugs and do not weigh on the back or belly band. A badly-balanced Governess Car or two-wheeled Dog Cart with heavy passengers on the rear seat will tip the vehicle, putting pressure on the horse's belly. This can be rectified, in the case of the Governess Car, by moving the passengers around until the proper balance is obtained. Some dog carts have a device so that the whole body of the vehicle can be moved to correct the balance, but unfortunately there are not many to be found now fitted with this appliance. Most of the dog cart off-shoots such as Village Carts and Ralli Cars have moveable seats which slide along runners on each side of the vehicle and are adjusted by means of a centre handle or bolts and slots under the seat. If a vehicle without a moveable seat is difficult to balance a weight can be carried on the floor and moved forward or backward until it is in the required position.

The ends of the shafts should be about level with the hames. If they are too far back the tip of the shaft may be pushed forward between the horse's shoulder and the collar. If they are too far forward the reins will keep getting caught up with the shafts and the horse will bang his nose on the shaft tips if he turns his head. There should be enough room between the horse's tail and the dashboard to prevent any danger of the vehicle hitting the animal on the hocks or rubbing his tail and, of course the shafts should be wide enough to accommodate the horse. Ones which are too narrow will quickly rub the animals' sides.

Once the Whip is satisfied that the horse is comfortable and calm, he can then trot on. The pace should be kept at a constant six to nine miles an hour depending on the length of the animal's stride. Nothing tires a horse more than incessant changes of pace and he should never be hustled out of that which is naturally the most comfortable for him.

The pace should be checked and the horse balanced before approaching a corner. It is very easy to bring a horse down on his side by turning too quickly or suddenly.

Changing Direction. A left turn can be executed by rounding the left wrist so that the back of the hand is inclined towards the body with the thumb downwards. This puts pressure on to the nearside rein and releases the offside rein sufficiently to bring round a light-mouthed, obedient horse. A right turn with such a horse can be made by turning the wrist so that the little finger is drawn upwards towards the body. This slackens the nearside rein and increases the tension on the offside rein. The beginner is usually inclined to swing his hands to the left or right in the direction of the turn – a bad fault and one that must be checked. The hands should not move from their position in the centre of the body.

With a less sensitive horse, however, the right hand will be needed to assist the left through a turn. Both reins remain in the left hand, but for a right turn the whole of the right hand is placed a little in front of the left and over the offside rein, the back of the hand uppermost. Pressure is then put on to the offside rein. A left turn is made in a similar manner with the right hand over the nearside rein. When the right hand is assisting the left the hands must be kept together and there should be no slack rein hanging between them.

If the horse is pulling, the right hand will again be needed to support the left. Used for this purpose, the hand is placed a little in front of the left one and over both reins. The nearside rein lies between the middle and third fingers and the offside rein goes under the little finger. The whip remains, at all times, in its usual position in the right hand.

To lengthen or shorten the reins, the right hand is placed in the same position. The contact on the horse's mouth is taken with the right hand and the required length of rein is pushed or pulled out from the left one.

Taking Out. The procedure for taking the horse out of the vehicle is the reverse to putting to. First the passengers dismount, then the Whip, who tucks the ends of the reins through the offside pad terret. The belly band is undone, breeching straps unbuckled and, last of all, the traces are unhooked. A check must be made to see that the ends of the reins are placed well in front of the tug stop before the vehicle is pushed back from the horse. If the reins become caught on the stop it is possible for the horse to receive a nasty jab in the mouth. It is better always to push the vehicle back from the horse rather than to lead him out of it. This last method can encourage the horse to creep forward, a habit that can lead to a broken shaft and a frightened horse should the former fall from the tugs.

Learning to Handle the Whip. Although the beginner may find holding reins and whip in the approved manner difficult at first, it soon enough becomes a matter of second nature. It is often helpful in the first stages if the whip is replaced by a small riding cane. This accustoms the newcomer to the feeling of holding a whip, without his having to worry about what the lash is doing and it is certainly preferable to starting without a stick of any kind.

Sleighing. Opportunities for sleighing in England are, unfortunately, infrequent. Ideal conditions only being obtainable if freezing temperatures follow a heavy fall of snow. Then, side roads, on which the snow has become packed by traffic, are ideal, if left unsalted.

For work in light sleighs, special shoes or studs are rarely necessary. A sensible horse soon learns to shorten his stride and lessen the chance of slipping. The use of knee pads and brushing boots is, however, a sensible precaution to take.

Harness for a single sleigh is the same as for a single vehicle, apart from the reins, which should be longer. Many sleighs are driven from a low seat, the reins passing from the saddle terrets and over a high rein rail, designed to prevent them from getting under the horse's tail, before they reach the Whip's hand. Tandem leader reins, though rather long, are often used in a sleigh rather than the usual single reins, which can be dangerously short.

When moving off, it is advisable to get the sleigh started before loading it down with passengers. It is easiest of all for the horse if even the Whip (dare I say it?) does not mount until after the sleigh is in motion. Once on the move, of course, it runs very easily.

Chapter 3

DRIVING A PAIR

Finding two horses or ponies which will go and look well as a pair can be an exhausting occupation, and matching an already proven single horse is often more difficult than finding two new ones from scratch.

The ideal pair should look and perform as one horse twice and be of matching colour and have virtually identical markings. Above all, they should be of the same breed or type. No matter how alike they may be in colour, if one is a heavy Welsh cob and the other a light Anglo-Arab they can never be called a true pair. It is unlike that two such horses so different in their action could ever move stride for stride. When seen from the front, the perfect pair should be of the same width and have similar shaped heads and from the box seat their quarters should match for breadth and height. When viewed from the side both horses must again be of equal proportion as regards length of body and height from the ground.

At the turn of the century, a pair horse vehicle was part of every large household and there was always a demand for matched pairs. A dealer's frequent trick, employed to sell two horses of different heights as a pair, was to put the taller horse on the nearside so that the dip in the road reduced his height by a couple of inches.

Most four-wheeled vehicles, and a few two-wheeled ones are suitable for pair driving. In both cases the horses are harnessed on either side of a central pole. With a four-wheeled vehicle the conventional pair horse harness is used, but when horses are driven to a two-wheeled vehicle either curricle or cape harness is necessary.

The most common vehicles now in use for driving a pair are four-wheelers, such as phaetons, waggonettes and types of dog carts.

Pair Harness. The harness and the method of harnessing a pair to such a vehicle is very similar to that employed for a

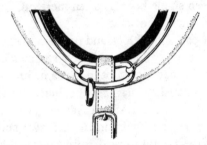

Fig. 14 Detail of collar and hames showing kidney link and ring

single horse. The harness on both animals of a pair must, of course, be identical, although the collars may be of a different size to ensure a proper fitting. The collar, as before, is put on first and the hames are fastened. These latter differ from those on single harness as they are joined at the bottom by a link, known as a kidney link on account of its shape (Fig. 14). On to the bottom half of this, lies a floating ring to which the pole chain or pole strap is fastened (Fig. 15). At the turn of the century it was traditional for pole chains to be used when a vehicle such as a mail phaeton was owner-driven, whilst pole straps were used when a landau or victoria was coachman-driven. The tops of the hames in each case are secured by the usual hame straps and both horses have those buckled so that the points of the straps face inwards. In case of accident, when it may be essential to release a trace, it is far quicker and more effective to undo the hame strap of either

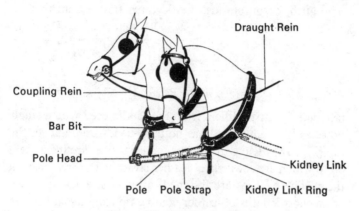

Fig. 15 Detail of pair put to

horse than to struggle with a trace tug buckle or try to unhook the trace from the vehicle. More purchase can be obtained if the point of the hame strap can be pulled downwards and away from the collar rather than upwards and towards the centre. It is very important that hame straps should be in new condition as they take a tremendous amount of strain when the pole comes forward. The pole pushes on the pole chains which, in turn, pull on the kidney link ring and hames, exerting a strong downward pressure on the top hame strap.

The false martingale is buckled right round the collar and through the top part of the kidney link as in Fig. 14. This method of buckling holds the hames on to the collar when pressure is put on to them by the movement of the pole, particularly when stopping or going down hills, and prevents the hames from being pulled off the collar.

Following the putting on of the collar, the pad, girth, back strap and crupper are placed on the back, the crupper is then placed under the tail and the pad lifted forward into position. The girth, incorporating the false martingale, can then be

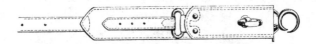

Fig. 16 Pair pad

fastened. The pad differs from the saddle used with a single horse as it is lighter and has no back-band running over the top (Fig. 16). Below the terrets, on each side, are metal dees on to which are sewn short leather straps with three holes in them. These straps are fastened to buckles which are sewn on to short lengths of leather coming up from metal dees on the top of the hame tug buckles (Fig. 17). Having buckled the

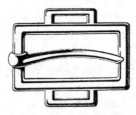

Fig. 17 Hame tug buckle for pair

hame tug buckle strap to the pad straps, the belly band is passed through the false martingale and fastened. The belly band buckles on to a strap which is sewn to a metal dee below the hame tug buckle (Fig. 18) and is left slightly looser than with single harness.

The traces are left lying over the horses' backs in readiness for putting to. The nearside horse has his nearside trace lying on top of his offside trace and the procedure is reversed for the offside horse.

Some pair harness incorporates breeching, but it is more frequently used with breast harness than with collars. In fact, a breast harness is not very safe unless it is used with breech-

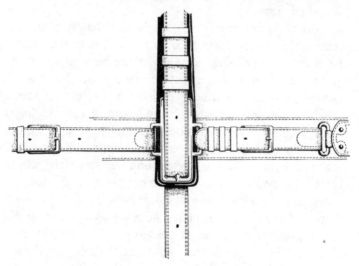

Fig. 18 Detail of pair pad showing tug buckle

ing. When breeching is fitted it is buckled alongside or under the traces to the hame tug buckle and then passes round the quarters to the tug buckle on the other side. It is held in place by a quarter strap which goes over the loins and through the back piece of the crupper. This quarter strap frequently has a loop below the breeching through which the traces pass. As the vehicle runs forward the pole, as we have seen, pulls on the collars which, in turn, bring forward the hame tug buckles and cause breeching to tighten round the quarters. The weight of the vehicle is then held by the quarters instead of being taken solely on the tops of the horses' necks.

When breeching is not used, trace bearers are often worn to prevent the traces from sagging. These resemble a loin strap and lie over the loin, passing through the back strap of the crupper. A loop is fitted on each end through which the traces are passed before being hooked on to the roller bolts or swingle tree.

Next the reins are fitted. Pair harness has two draught reins which go from the outsides of the bits to the Whip's hand and two coupling reins which are buckled on to the draught reins at a point about 24 inches from the hand. A number of oval-shaped holes punched at one-inch intervals along the draught reins enable the length of the couplings, which are fastened to the inside of the bits, to be altered quite easily from the box seat. The coupling rein, which is buckled to the left draught rein, is buckled on to the left of the offside horse's bit and that which is fastened to the right draught rein goes to the right side of the near horse's bit. This means that when the left rein is pulled both horses will turn to the left, as pressure is put on to the left sides of both mouths (Fig. 19). The nearside rein should be the rein which does NOT have the little buckle at the end of it. It is very dangerous to have the buckle on the nearside rein because, when the horses are put to, the nearside rein will be thrown over their backs to the offside in preparation for mounting. If a buckle hits someone it may cause an injury and it is there-fore far safer to toss the non-buckle end of the rein across to the offside. Another good reason for keeping to the rule of the buckle rein on the offside is that, when harnessing the horses, the correct rein is always put on to the right horse. Once coupling reins are carefully adjusted it is most annoying to find the wrong reins have been put on and so rendered all the previous adjustments useless. When the reins are put on during harnessing, they are passed through the pad and hame terrets and the loose end, beyond the coupling buckle, is tucked through the back-piece or pad terret.

The bridle is put on last, the draught rein being buckled to the outside of the bit. The coupling rein is then passed

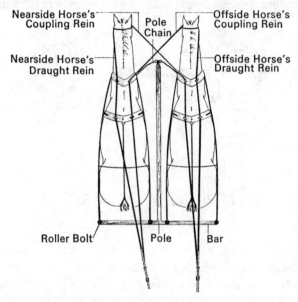

Fig. 19 Coupling reins

through the noseband and the billet of the rein put through its keeper in preparation for putting to. If the horses and vehicle are elegant and the occasion dressy, Buxton bits (Fig. 20) can be used, but when the vehicle is of a sporting kind then Liverpool bits with a bar across the bottom are considered to be the most suitable. This bar is important as it prevents the horses getting the bit cheeks hooked up in the coupling reins or in each others' bridles.

If Liverpool bits are used the kind with fixed mouthpieces are preferable as the sideways pull from the coupling reins can turn the rings on moveable mouthpieces, pressing them against the sides of the horses' jaws, causing discomfort and probably head-shaking.

In order to get an even feel on both horses' mouths it is often found necessary to buckle one horse on to cheek and the

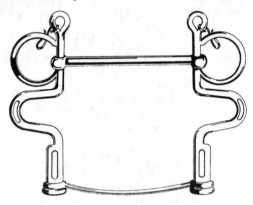

Fig. 20 Buxton bit

other on to middle bar. It is far more comfortable for all concerned if both horses can be bitted so that they go evenly. One horse might wear an elastic curb chain and the other a chain one, but it may take months of experimenting before a complete solution is found.

Putting to. Before putting to the vehicle should be drawn into a good position for driving off. The pole chains or straps can then be put on to the pole head and the pole pin secured. At this point it is as well to check that the locking plate is well greased. One which is dried up will make the vehicle unpleasant to drive, causing the pole to jerk from side to side and to jump about to such an extent that the horses are almost hit in the teeth by its untoward movements. A dry plate also makes the vehicle difficult to steer.

As each horse is put to he is led from behind the vehicle towards and alongside the pole. He should not be backed into position in case he hits the splinter bar. The pole chain is then hooked on to the floating ring on the kidney link and the outside trace should always be fixed first. This ensures that the horse cannot swing his quarters out from the vehicle. If the inside trace is hooked first he is able to swing right round, being held to his vehicle by the inside trace and pole chain. In those circumstances a panicky horse and an accident are likely to ensue. When the horse is being taken out the outside trace must be undone *last*. The inside trace has to be attached quickly and carefully and to do so necessitates leaning behind the horse. If one of the horses is likely to kick he should be put to first and his inside trace secured from the pole side in preference to leaning across his hind legs. Never must the trace be fixed by someone climbing between the horses and the vehicle, however quiet the animals may be. In practice it will be found that the pole chains tend to keep the horses near to the pole.

Should the vehicle have a solid splinter bar a greater amount of collar pressure will be exerted on the outer sides of the necks, but by shortening the inside traces to get the collar lying evenly this can be overcome. As the traces will need to be shortened only by about 1 inch, and the distance between trace holes is usually $1\frac{1}{2}$ inches or more, a small problem arises. An effective method of overcoming the difficulty is to wrap layers of thick leather round the inside roller bolts. This makes a greater distance for the traces to pass round and thus shortens them to the required amount. It is also preferable to punching a series of holes in the traces and avoids having the wrong trace put on to the wrong set of harness. If swingle trees can be used they are better than a solid splinter bar. With a swingle tree attachment the traces can give and take with the action and the collars will be flat on the shoulders. A solid bar makes the horse work first on one shoulder and then on the other, thus pulling on alternate traces.

Each pole chain is now hooked to its correct length. If a chain with a hook at each end is used, one end of the chain is hooked on to the pole head and the other is passed from the pole through the floating ring on the kidney link and then hooked down on to the chain near the pole head on the side which is farthest from the pole. The back of the hook should be uppermost so that it cannot get caught in the bar of the bits. The chains should, however, be loose enough to allow some play in the pole. If they are too tight they will pull continuously on the horses' necks and cause considerable discomfort. On the other hand it is very important to see that they are tight enough to prevent the splinter bar or the swingle trees from touching the horses' hocks when they are going down a hill.

The coupling reins are buckled next, the horse with the highest head carriage having his on top. A ring can be threaded on to the reins to keep them together where they cross and prevent the coupling from getting caught on the pole head.

Having put to, it is advisable to walk right round the turn-out before mounting to make certain that all is in order. A check should be made that the pole pin is in place and that all four traces are satisfactorily secured. If swingle trees fitted with leather pieces (sometimes called rat rails), to prevent the traces from sliding off, are used, check that these are threaded through and also see that the pole chains have been hooked to the right length. Finally, be certain to look at the coupling reins to ensure that they have been buckled on to the correct place. It has been known for an inexperienced groom to buckle the coupling reins to their own bits. The potential disaster here can be imagined.

Mounting Procedure. The reins are taken in the left hand from their position by the offside terret. Standing by the off-side front wheel, the reins are held level, with the nearside rein over the index finger and the offside rein under the middle finger. The offside rein then is pulled out about a foot and both reins are passed into the right hand but one finger lower down. This leaves the index finger and thumb free to grasp the hand loop on the vehicle. If the vehicle is a large one, such as a brake, the way to mount is to place the left foot on the wheel plate of the hub, the right foot on the roller bolt, then the left foot on the step and the right foot on the foot-board. With vehicles of different varieties these directions may have to be modified. The reins are then passed back to the left hand and the apron wrapped round as the Whip sits down. The whip is taken in the right hand. The lash of a pair whip is slightly longer than that of a single whip. This is to enable the nearside horse, who is a greater distance away from the Whip than a single horse, to be reached with ease.

Driving a pair of well-trained and properly put-together animals is no more difficult than driving a single horse. The principles are the same and the methods described in the chapter on single harness for handling the reins also apply to a pair. The main difference is that the reins spread more from the fingers and there is more weight, particularly if both horses begin to pull. Both animals must be made to do their fair share of the work. Ideally, they should move exactly out of step when they trot. As the nearside horse's off fore leg and near hind leg touch the ground, so the offside horse's near fore leg and off hind leg also touch the ground. In practice, one horse of the pair usually assumes the role of leader and the other puts himself into rhythm in the way just described.

The difficulty arises when two unschooled horses are put to by the beginner who has little or no knowledge of driving a pair or of how to adjust the coupling reins to advantage.

Moving Off. The brake of the vehicle, which should be on before starting, must be taken off with some subtlety just before the horses are to be asked to move off. It is considered bad form to release the brake with a clatter and, this apart, the noise will be heard by the horses who will soon take it as a signal to leap into action. The horses should move off, as one, when given the office. If one is inclined to idleness and the other over-keen, care must be taken that they do not start off in a series of see-saw movements. It is sometimes a help if the over-anxious one is restrained by a man on foot until the lazy horse has put some weight into his collar; then both horses will start the vehicle together. If this is not done the keener animal will get into the habit of starting the vehicle on his own, towing his partner along with him. This is just the sort of thing that can lead to broken traces and strained hind legs or back, particularly if the vehicle is heavy or stuck in a muddy patch. When the command to walk on is given both horses should lean into their collars together. Once in draught a check should be made to see that the traces and pole chains are the right length and the couplings should be noted to see that they are satisfactory in relation to the way in which the horses are going on that particular day. Often, coupling which seemed all right on one day will appear wrong on the next, although the horses, vehicle and Whip are all the same.

The Coupling Reins. The secret of pair horse driving lies mainly in the coupling reins. The first thing to remember is that the pole chain tends to bring the horses together, so care must be taken to see that the coupling reins are tight enough to maintain an even pressure on each side of the horses' mouths. If the coupling reins are too long all the contact will be taken on the outsides of their mouths by the draught reins. If the coupling reins are too short, both animals will be forced to go with their heads turned inwards and each rein should then be let out a couple of holes to allow them to go slightly apart. The aim is to have both horses going with their heads straight and both doing their share of work. The collars should be level, with an equal tension on all four traces. Some very intelligent horses learn to keep their traces taut without actually doing any work, leaving all the pulling for their unfortunate companion. A watch must be kept for this and corrective action taken. The best way of seeing whether or not an animal is working is to observe the muscles over his back. When a horse pulls into his traces his quarter muscles bulge and ripple. If he is not working, his quarters just swing from side to side as he jogs happily along. Of course this can only apply to going up hills or pulling a load on grass. On a level road he may be doing his share without appearing to be making any special effort.

If both horses are exactly the same size and height and carry their heads in precisely the same position, the coupling reins will be buckled on similar holes on the draught reins, but if, for instance, the nearside horse has a long neck, carrying his head with his nose sticking *forwards*, and the offside horse has a short thick neck and tucks his head into his chest, then the couplings must be adjusted so that both horses are working evenly. A pair going in this manner, with both couplings on the centre holes of the draught reins, will mean that the offside horse is doing all the work. He will go forward until he is restricted by pressure from the bit, so this must be corrected by shortening his coupling rein on the left draught rein by, say, five holes. Pressure will then be put on to the left side of his bit, but will leave the right side of his bit loose. To rectify this, the right draught rein is shortened in the hand, which puts pressure on to the coupling rein of the nearside horse (the long-necked one), which appears to be the last thing that should be done, as it brings him to the right. But if his coupling rein is then let out the same number of holes along the right draught rein and the left draught rein is lengthened from the hand, matters are put right. By letting one horse out and bringing the other one in, both horses should then be level in their collars. It should be remembered that when starting from scratch, with both coupling reins buckled to the centre holes of the draught reins, if one coupling is adjusted upwards then the other should be adjusted the same number of holes downwards, otherwise the distance from the pole cannot be maintained.

Some reins have three holes at the billet end which are used for altering the length of draught and coupling reins. The main disadvantage of this arrangement is that they are likely to get buckled by mistake on the wrong hole, thus altering the coupling of the pair.

Another disadvantage of coupling reins is that a rein aid to one horse cannot be applied without the other animal being affected by it. If one of a pair is newly broken, or liable to some evasion, it is a help to put a pair of single reins to his bit as well as the coupling and draught reins. This single pair can be held loosely with the comforting thought that, should an emergency arise, something can immediately be done to correct the offender.

Hills and Corners. Hills should be descended with great care and the pace kept slow, the brake being used with discretion. When applying the brake the whip should be held in the left hand, with the reins, to leave the right hand free to work the brake lever. A watch is kept on the pole chains and as soon as the pole runs forward enough to tighten the chains, a little pressure is put on to the brake, more pressure being applied as necessary.

Corners should be approached slowly, remembering that the outside horse on the turn has to lengthen his stride to get round his partner. If the turn is taken too quickly, he will have to hurry to get round and may fall or slip.

Sometimes horses start to lean towards or away from the pole. As prevention is better and easier to cope with than cure, it is advisable to change the horses over fairly frequently before they learn this disagreeable habit.

Dual-purpose Vehicles. As mentioned earlier, some two-wheeled vehicles have a pole, instead of shafts, so that a pair may be driven to them. The best known is probably the Curricle, which was built solely for pair horse driving, although it was occasionally used with a team. Curricle harness can be used for driving a pair to various vehicles, such as dog carts and ralli cars which have been built or adapted for a pair. Quite a number of these vehicles are to be found throughout the country, which were built with a pole instead of shafts so that they could take a pair, and some were constructed so that they could easily be converted to take a pole or shafts as required. This meant that only one vehicle had to be housed to provide a variety of ways of driving. With the shafts on, either a single or tandem could be driven, or even a random (that is, three horses each one in front of the other). With a pole replacing the shafts, a pair, unicorn or team of ponies might be driven from a reasonably high dog cart.

Curricle Harness. Curricle harness has the same bridles, reins, collars and hames as the usual pair harness, but the pads are replaced by heavier driving saddles which have the pair-horse tug method of fixing the trace tug buckles to the pad. Between the rein terrets on the centre of each pad is a terret which has two rolling bolts across the centre. This terret is fixed so that it lies fore and aft, instead of widthways like the usual terrets. The curricle bar, which is made of steel, rests through these bolts across both horses' backs, and is free to roll a few inches to either side. When the horses are put to and standing at their usual distance away from the pole there should be about 6 inches of free curricle bar protruding from each side of the centre terrets. This allows some play if the horses part. At the ends of the bar there is a nut, held in position by a pin, to ensure that the bar cannot run right out of its terrets. In the centre of the curricle bar is an oval loop through which lies a stout strap. This strap is passed round a sprung attachment under the pole and secured by means of a strong double buckle. The weight of the pole and the balance of the vehicle lies in the adjustment of this strap. The spring under the pole helps to prevent the horses from getting sore backs. Once the vehicle is going along a level surface, if it has been correctly balanced, there should not be any weight on the horses' backs. Heavy saddles are worn to guard against the time when the vehicle is not properly balanced, such as going down hills, or before and when the Whip, passengers and tiger mount. Under those circumstances, the horses take the weight of the unbalanced vehicle by the pole through the bar on their backs.

When putting to, it is most important to see that the traces are of the correct length. If they are too long the horses will draw the vehicle by the curricle bar and they will soon be made sore by the rear of their harness saddles.

A precautionary strap to prevent the cart from tipping backwards can be added to the harness. This is a long strap with a buckle at each end and is fastened to the outside girth strap of one horse, passed under his belly, up over the pole and under the belly of the other horse, before being buckled on to his outside girth strap.

A principal disadvantage of the curricle method of putting to is that if one horse should fall he will probably drag his partner down with him, owing to the bar being fixed to the pads.

Cape Cart Method. Another way of harnessing a pair to a two-wheeled vehicle is known as the Cape Cart harness method. The horses are harnessed to the pole by means of a yoke which carries the latter (Fig. 21). A vehicle adapted for

Fig. 21 Detail of Cape harness

Cape harness has a longer pole than one for curricle harness so that the yoke can be fixed about 18 inches inwards from the end. Breast harness is worn with Cape harness, and breeching is essential to prevent the vehicle from hitting the horses when going down hills or stopping. Breeching and breast harness are fitted in the same way as already described for normal pair-horse driving and bridles and coupling reins are the same. The pads in this case take no weight so they can be light; all the weight of the unbalanced vehicle is taken by the yoke through the yoke straps and is carried by the horses over a padded piece of leather in front of their withers. The yoke is about 5 feet long and is made from a piece of lance wood about 1 inch in diameter. It can be fixed to the pole by means of a short leather strap with a ring at each end. This strap lies over the pole and the yoke is passed through the rings allowing a certain amount of sideways play. The centre of the yoke, at the point where the pole, the strap and rings come into contact with it, is covered with a layer of leather to prevent wear in the wood. The yoke is fastened to the horses' necks by straps passing from the centre of the yoke, near the pole, over the neck, alongside the strap holding the breast harness, through the loops on the padded leather piece in front of the withers and then down to the outside ends of the yoke where they are buckled. The horses are poled up in the usual way with pole straps going from dees on the centre of their breast collars to the pole head.

Chapter 4

TANDEM DRIVING

Tandem driving originated hundreds of years ago when a lead horse was harnessed in front of the animal between the shafts to assist in hauling a heavily laden vehicle through the mud or when tackling a steep ascent. During snowy weather it was quite usual for the two-wheeled Royal Mail cart to be pulled by a tandem on its journey to isolated villages.

Tandem clubs were formed towards the middle of the nineteenth century and a number of matches were run between vehicles horsed in this fashion.

Tandem carts were built with extremely high box seats, possibly to accentuate the skill of the young bloods who drove tandems of well-bred horses. The cocking cart, which was used to take cocks to cockfighting contests, was an example of this trend.

The enthusiasm shown by the Prince of Wales for daring driving inspired others to try their hand at the sport. He even went one better and drove a randem, and history relates that he drove one from London to Brighton in four and a half hours.

Before the advent of motor horse boxes it was a common practice to take a hunter to the meet in the lead of a tandem. Harnessed in front, he could jog on gently without exhausting himself. On arrival, he was mounted and the groom was left to return home with the shaft horse and vehicle.

The word 'wheeler' used to refer solely to either of the rearmost horses in a team. It is now also used when referring to the shaft horse in a tandem.

The quotation of a late nineteenth-century horse dealer delightfully sums up tandem driving 'I always look upon a man as drives a tandem a fool; he makes two hosses do the work of one and most likely breaks his silly neck.' Nevertheless, for anyone wanting to progress from driving a single and pair, and who is still in search of thrills and excitement, tandem driving is the answer. Things can go very wrong with lightning speed, but when they go well there is nothing to compare with the pleasure obtained from sitting up behind free-moving horses, harnessed in tandem and going well into their bits. It requires a light, sensitive hand on the reins and an alert brain to produce a successful tandem. Indeed, the touch required is so delicate that it has been compared with playing a harp.

In some ways, driving a tandem is more difficult than driving a team. Whereas the leaders of a team balance each other, there is nothing but the skill of the Whip to prevent a tandem leader from turning right round and facing the cart. For most lady Whips, who are ambitious to get hold of four reins, a tandem is more suitable than a team. The weight of team reins alone is enough to exhaust the average lady unless she is extremely fit and accustomed to team driving, although anyone who can drive a tandem competently could get up behind a well-mannered team and take them for a short distance in reasonable safety.

The principles of driving a team resemble those pertaining to a tandem. In both cases four reins are used and the methods of handling them are similar. It would be difficult for a newcomer to team driving to take a team for a long journey as it is unlikely that the muscles in his left forearm and fingers would be strong enough to drive them for any distance, particularly if they started to pull. Apart from the extra weight, there is also a wider pull from the reins of a

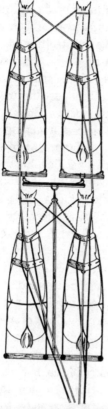

Fig. 22 Reins on a team

team. Team reins have couplings like a pair (Fig. 22); they spread more from the Whip's hand, stretching the fingers slightly. Tandem reins have a straighter pull from the box to the wheeler's terrets and are, therefore, closer together and less tiring to hold.

Almost any two horses who already go quietly in single harness, and who are mentally compatible, should go in tandem without much trouble. It is, however, essential that the leader must learn to go on freely without the support of shafts. Assuming that he was broken correctly, he will be accustomed to walking and trotting ahead on long reins, so no problems should arise when he is asked to go into the lead of tandem. It is, nevertheless, inadvisable to attempt to put horses into tandem until they are thoroughly reliable in single harness. Finding horses that will look and go well in tandem is easier than searching for a matching pair. The leader can be a better bred, showier animal than the wheeler. He may even be an inch or two smaller, but he must go freely on, without constant nagging, be absolutely traffic-proof and neither shy violently nor kick. The wheeler should be the ideal gig horse with a long free stride, knowing his job thoroughly. He can then be left to get on with it if things go wrong with the leader and can be trusted not to kick or jib. Nothing demoralizes a leader more than a kicking wheeler and such animals should be avoided at all costs.

Almost any two-wheeled vehicle with a high box seat can be used for tandem driving. The best vehicle, probably, is a two-wheeled dog cart, but unfortunately these are not easily found. Vehicles with a low box are to be avoided since nothing is so uncomfortable as driving a tandem from a low seat. The leader can neither be seen nor controlled properly and the angle of the reins is made too straight. Adequate extra height can often be achieved by adding another cushion or two to a box seat which would otherwise be a little too low. Most high gigs are suitable but four-wheeled vehicles are not to be recommended for the beginner. If, with a four-wheeler, the leader should come round to face the Whip, the vehicle will probably articulate, as the shaft horse comes round, and is then likely to turn over, whereas a two-wheeled vehicle can be brought round rapidly and still remain upright. The leader can then be extricated from the muddle which he has helped to cause.

Learning the Art. The best way to learn how to drive a tandem is to sit on the box seat alongside an expert and watch every move he makes. Then, still accompanied by that expert, the beginner can take the reins behind a well-trained, free-moving tandem and have a try. It can be frustrating to find that the moment the reins are transferred from the hands of the expert to those of the beginner the once free-moving, dead-straight tandem becomes a straggling mess resembling a pair, but with perseverance the art can be acquired.

Having experienced the feeling of four reins, it is a help to go home and set up two pairs of reins on to the backs of two chairs, one in front of the other. These can be fixed so that the chairs balance on their rear legs, being tied to something solid so that they do not tip right over. Then, sitting on a chair on top of a table, the Whip can practise turns, loops and a variety of experiments that will make the holding of four reins a matter of second nature. It is important to be thoroughly conversant with the order of the reins in the hand so that any required rein may be instantly located. A small cane should be held during these practice sessions to ensure that the right hand gets accustomed to holding the whip as well as to manipulating four reins. After these exercises the beginner's reactions will be improved noticeably when next he has the chance of getting at the real thing.

Tandem Harness. The harness for tandem is very simple. The shaft horse wears the same harness that he would for single gig work with four additions. His bridle carries tandem wheeler, also known as leading eye, rosettes (Fig. 23) instead of plain ones. These differ from the latter by being fitted with a ring protruding outwards on each side of the browband, through which the leader's reins pass on their way

Fig. 23 Tandem wheeler rosette

to the Whip's hand. The wheeler's bit, if it is a curb such as a Liverpool, has a bar across the bottom joining the two cheeks. This will prevent the wheeler from getting his bit hooked over a lead rein and so, inadvertently, giving the leader the office to make a sharp turn. The hame tug buckles have a metal eye on the under side (Fig. 24) on to which the leader's

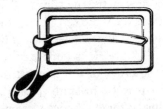

Fig. 24 Tandem wheeler hame tug buckle

traces, or tandem bar traces, are hooked. The saddle terrets are divided in half by bars with rollers on them (Fig. 25) and are known as roller bar terrets. The wheeler's reins go below this bar and the leader's reins above. The bars prevent the leader and wheeler reins from sticking together, a circumstance which could result in a horse being pulled in the wrong direction. The leader's harness is usually very light. His bridle should match that of the wheeler in stitching, winker shape and buckle design. Browband fronts, crests, and similar trimmings should be identical. A breast collar is

Fig. 25 Wheeler terret

frequently used on the leader, though this is purely a matter of personal choice. The saddle is lighter than that of the wheeler and has no back band or belly band and there are leather loops fixed on each side (Fig. 26) through which the

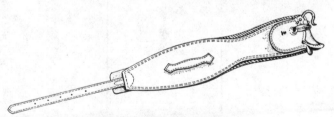

Fig. 26 Tandem leader saddle

lead traces pass. Hanging from the back piece of the crupper is a loin strap with trace bearers, two leather loops which buckle on the loin strap and hold the traces up. In this way the traces are prevented from hanging down and getting entangled in the leader's hind legs or the wheeler's fore legs. The leader's traces are about 3 feet longer than normal gig traces and have spring cock eyes (Fig. 27) at the ends which are clipped on to the wheeler's hame tug eyelets. If tandem bars are used the leader has normal gig traces. Some tandem bars

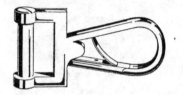

Fig. 27 Spring cock eye

owned by the author (Fig. 28) consist of a wheeler bar, which is 1 foot 11 inches long and a leader bar of 2 feet 5 inches. The wheeler bar has a round metal eye at each end on to

Fig. 28 Tandem bars

which are sewn two lengths of trace 1 foot 10 inches long with a spring cock eye at the end of each. The hooks (cock eyes) are fixed to the wheeler's hame tug buckle eyes. In the centre of this bar is a small length of chain 9 inches long with a spring hook on the end, which is hooked on to a ring on the wheeler's bottom hame strap, or hame chain, alongside the false martingale. This prevents the bars from falling on to the wheeler's fore legs. Also, from the centre of the wheeler bar, but facing forwards, is a large open hook on to which the leader's bar is hooked and secured by means of a small leather strap and buckle. The leader bar consists of a light swingle tree with the usual trace hooks at each end and a ring in the centre that goes over the large hook on the wheeler bar just mentioned. When using bars, care should be taken to ensure that the hook on the centre, attaching the wheel and lead bars together, is always secured by the little strap. Otherwise the bar on the wheeler's bit may become caught on the hook.

For the sake of uniformity, bars should be painted and lined out to correspond with the vehicle. If the cart is varnished, then the bars should be the same, whilst the metal work of the hooks and fittings should match that of the harness furniture and the lamps and handles on the vehicle.

The measurements given above are suitable for animals of about 14·2 h.h. but would, of course, be different for smaller or larger animals.

The use of bars, instead of long traces, makes tandem driving far easier for the beginner. Horses can be turned in a narrow road with ease whereas, without bars, the traces can hang in a loop, touch the ground and be a source of trouble.

Putting To. When putting to, the wheeler is put to first in the same way that has already been described for single horse. If tandem bars are used they are put on to the wheeler as soon as he has been put to. The leader is then led into position in front of the wheeler and his traces are passed through the loops on his pad if this has not been done before he was led out of the stable. It is often easier to have the traces through the pad loops and left lying over his back, or coiled round themselves in a figure-eight loop, and hooked back on to the pad terrets if long lead traces are used, before bringing him out of the stable. He can then be put to more quickly and with less fuss. The traces go through the trace bearers before being hooked on to the leader's bar or wheeler's hame tugs, as the case may be. The leader's reins go through his hame and pad terrets, pass through the wheeler's bridle terrets and finally through the upper part of the wheeler's pad terrets before being folded with the wheel reins and looped over the wheel horse's back. The lead reins do not pass through the wheeler's hame terrets and it is not usual to buckle the leader's reins.

Having put to, both horses can be held by one assistant. The procedure is to stand on the offside, alongside the wheeler's head. The left hand can control the wheeler while the right hand rests on the leader's reins. On no account should a tandem be put to, or driven, without an active assistant.

Having put to, the Whip is advised to walk round the turn-out, as usual, to check that all is to his liking. The leader at this stage should be standing so that his traces hang in a slight loop. The reins can then be taken on the offside in the right hand. Then, with the Whip standing alongside the step of the vehicle and taking care not to make any contact with the horses' mouths, the reins can be transferred into the left hand in the correct driving position (Fig. 29). The nearside leader rein is placed over the index finger and the offside leader rein goes under the index finger. The nearside wheeler rein is put below the offside lead rein, above the middle finger, and the offside wheeler rein lies under the middle finger. They are gripped in this position, as they lie together in the palm of the hand, by pressure from the third and fourth fingers. The reins should be adjusted evenly and then the off-side reins can be lengthened by about 4 inches, so that when the Whip reaches the box seat they will all be level. Immediately before mounting the reins are once more transferred to the right hand, being held in the same order but one finger

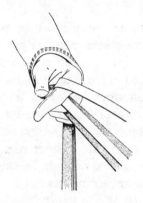

Fig. 29 Holding reins for tandem or team driving

lower down so that the right index finger and thumb are free to hold the rail when mounting. As soon as the box seat is reached, the reins are taken into the left hand and immediately checked to ensure that they are level. When he first drives a tandem the beginner will find it a great help if his instructor makes a slight scratch mark on each rein exactly where they should be held for those particular horses when they are trotting straight on a level surface. These marks are a tremendous asset in keeping the horses going with the right amount of slack leader trace.

Having reached the box seat, the sitting position must be considered. It is a mistake to achieve a high driving posture by leaning or almost standing against the seat. Both methods are dangerous because if a horse should peck or fall the Whip will probably be pulled from his precarious perch. It is essential that a comfortable sitting position should be adopted with the back of the box seat no more than 4 inches higher than the front. The feet must be planted firmly on the footrest or floor.

Moving Off. Once the whip has been taken in the right hand and the apron adjusted round the knees, the horses may be given the warning, by a gentle feel on their mouths, that they will be required to move off. It is best to indicate by a nod to the assistant when he should let go of their heads rather than risk a verbal command 'let 'em go' becoming an office to the horses to walk on a fraction before it is required of them. If they are wearing quarter rugs, these should be removed gently, without a flourish. In tandem driving it is starting off with an unyielding, heavy hand which can cause trouble. If, for instance, the leader is a considerably better bred and therefore more sensitive horse than the wheeler, the Whip must start his tandem with extreme care. With a beginner at the ribbons when the command 'walk on' is given to such a tandem team the leader will leap into immediate action whilst his companion remains stationary. A second or two later the slower reacting wheeler moves forward, but not before the leader, having felt a dead pull on his traces, has stopped. The wheeler, now in motion, then ploughs forward into his leader, hitting the latter's quarters with the point of the shaft. Not surprisingly such liberties can cause the leader to jump forward, and he may set to kicking, thus breaking a bar or trace. Such are the excitements which can arise when neither the Whip nor his horses are very experienced in the art of tandem.

In order to avoid such a performance, make certain that the wheeler starts the vehicle a fraction of a second before the leader is allowed to move. This is a transition which calls for the utmost delicacy on the part of the Whip. Once the vehicle is gently rolling the active assistant can jump in alongside the Whip.

The Leader's Role. The most important thing to remember about tandem driving is that the leader should be kept out of his work, though up to his bit, at all times, other than when going up hills, when he can be called upon to assist the wheeler. If the leader pulls at the traces all the time, the poor wheeler feels as though he is being towed along, rather like someone who is being pulled by the hand of another who can run faster. Anyone who has experienced this unpleasant feeling can sympathize with a wheeler in such a predicament. Worried because he is being pulled by the leader and in danger of falling, he starts to hang back. Then a tug-of-war is on between the wheeler and the leader. This state of affairs can end in one of two ways: either the wheeler is pulled on to his nose or, in an effort to retain his balance, he finishes up sitting on his hocks with his collar half-way up his neck.

Turning a Tandem. The reins must always stay in the left hand and NEVER be moved from their initial position. The right hand carries the whip and can be used to assist the left as required. It is simplest to keep the right hand in position over the reins, a couple of inches in front of its partner so that immediate action is possible. The third and fourth fingers of the right hand lie over the offside reins, the middle finger goes over the near wheel rein and the index finger is placed over the near lead rein. The offside reins can often be treated as one. To incline the horses across the road to the

63

right, as when overtaking a stationary object, the little and third fingers of the right hand are pressed down on both off-side reins, an action which will cause leader and wheeler to incline to the right. An incline to the left is obtained by turning the left hand so that the thumb goes downwards towards the body, thus tightening the near lead rein, and at the same time pressure is put on the nearside wheel rein with the middle finger of the right hand.

It is essential to slow and balance the horses before any sharp turns are made. Modern roads are extremely slippery and an unbalanced turn may end in a fall. The horses should be up to their bits going at an even and slow trot with the leader well out of his work. If the leader is pulling on the traces, the wheeler will not be able to turn the vehicle. For a sharp turn it is often easiest to loop a lead rein. Let us consider how a sharp turn to the right down a side road can be made by this means.

When the leader has reached the centre of the road which he is going to be asked to turn down, a loop is taken in the offside lead rein by catching up about 4 inches of the rein with the right hand and securing it between the forefinger and thumb of the left hand (Fig. 30). This effectively brings the leader to the right, but it is something which needs to be carried out with some dexterity. Simultaneously, the near-side wheel rein must be held in opposition by pressure from the middle finger of the right hand to ensure that the wheeler does not cut his corner. Once the leader has turned, the loop must be dropped, otherwise he will keep on turning and end up facing his Whip. Next, the pressure on the nearside wheeler rein of opposition is removed and the wheeler is allowed to follow the leader round. If the wheeler does not turn quickly enough, a little pressure can be put on the off-side wheel rein with the little finger of the right hand. The reason for looping, is to leave the right hand free to assist the left as required.

A method of turning to the right without looping is as follows. First, catch up the nearside wheel rein with the middle finger of the right hand and, still holding it, slide the hand back a couple of inches over the other reins towards the left hand. This puts considerable contact on to the left side

Fig. 30 Looping a Rein

of the wheeler's mouth in opposition to the turn to the right. Then, turn the right hand down so that both offside reins are tightened by pressure from the third and little fingers. The leader will then turn to the right followed gently by the wheeler. If the leader does not come round quickly enough the back of the left hand can be turned down, the thumb going away from the body. This action will relieve the pressure, caused by the turn, on the left side of his mouth and allow him round smoothly.

A sharp turn to the left is made by looping the nearside leader rein to bring the leader round and opposing the offside reins with the right hand.

Light-mouthed, active horses can be brought round a

gentle turn by rounding and dropping the left hand to left or right. A little help from the right hand where required is all that is necessary for a skilful turn.

Any inclination for the horses not to go in a straight line can be rectified by either shortening or lengthening the two centre reins. If the leader tends to go to the right and the wheeler to the left, for example, a loosening of the central reins will immediately straighten them. Equally, if the leader wanders to the left and the wheeler to the right, tightening the centre reins will have the desired effect.

Reins should be shortened or lengthened by placing the right hand in front of the left, taking the contact on the horses' mouths and then pushing or pulling the required amount of rein through the left hand from the front to the back.

There is a tendency for the nearside wheel rein to slip because, instead of being secured singly between gloved fingers, it is alongside the offside lead rein which may cause it to slide out of position. One remedy for this is to sit on the end of it, a method which is also a help to the beginner when he is searching frantically for the elusive near wheel rein.

Up and Down Hills. When a steep downward hill has to be negotiated the leader must be kept back with his traces hanging in a large loop. Any pulling from him will start the wheeler slipping in his efforts to hold the cart back and may end in him being pulled down on to the road. To bring the leader well out of his work a loop can be taken in both lead reins, the loop being dropped on reaching the bottom of the hill. When a hill is to be climbed the lead reins should be lengthened by pulling the required amount of rein out from the left hand with the right, thus enabling the leader to help the wheeler in pulling the vehicle up the hill. He must not, be allowed to pull too hard or his traces will come up above his back.

Should the leader turn unexpectedly it is best to adopt the policy of 'follow my leader' and let the wheeler go round, sorting out the direction of progression afterwards. If the wheeler is prevented from following on, the leader, almost inevitably, ends up side by side with the wheeler, his head to the latter's tail and with a broken trace into the bargain. The wheeler should be backed a step or two if possible during the manœuvre as this prevents a greater muddle.

Using the Whip. Skilful use of the whip is essential for successful tandem driving. A tandem whip has a stick about 5 feet long and a thong of approximately 8 feet and the whole should be light and well balanced. A heavy, badly balanced whip makes the wrist ache. When the whip is not in use the thong should be caught in a large loop, hanging down about 30 inches from just below the quill. The rest of the thong is twisted round the stick, the end being held under the right thumb. Catching or folding a thong should be achieved on foot before it is attempted from a box seat. The best way to accomplish this necessary feat is to draw a large S on a wall with chalk. Now, standing well back from the wall, hold the whip in the right hand with the lash secured under the right thumb and starting from the bottom left hand side follow the S with the top of the stick. Then, raise the stick from right to left and swing it to the right. Quickly drop the stick and catch the thong with an upward wrist action. With considerable practice this will catch the thong on the stick. Drop the stick to an horizontal position across the body and hold it, half-way along, with the thumb of the left hand, so as to leave the right one free to wind up the rest of the thong. The whip is then returned to the right hand.

When driving the leader is hit by uncoiling the thong and hitting from the right side, inscribing a half-circle and landing the lash on the hock or flank. The thong is caught up afterwards by raising the whip upwards to a perpendicular position and by grasping the thong, or preferably the lash, either in the right hand or under the arm before folding as described above. As can be imagined, a good deal of practice on the ground in touching up an imaginary leader and catching the thong is required, otherwise passengers' hats will be removed and it is more than likely that the wheeler will receive that intended for his companion.

From the foregoing the aspiring tandem Whip will realize the importance of having a free-moving leader who will make it unnecessary to put the whip into use except on infrequent occasions.

The wheeler is hit by using the double thong, which is hanging from the stick, either between the collar pad or just behind the pad.

It is necessary to shorten the reins before using the whip as the right hand is so occupied with catching the thong that it is not readily available to assist the left in moments of crisis.

Chapter 5

TRAINING – THE EARLY STAGES

Those concerned with the training of horses rarely agree in every detail on the method by which they achieve the end product. Different ways are applied with varying degrees of success. The sequence described has been used by the author on a variety of horses and it is offered as a rough guide. Most horses will go in harness if the trainer has adequate time and patience.

A training routine should be established at the outset so that the young horse knows when he will be working and when he is free to rest. If he is never certain when he is to be taken out he may become tense and nervy and go off his food, so the lessons should take place at the same time each day, two short sessions being always preferable to one long one. Each lesson should be planned in advance with the object of either teaching the horse something new or of establishing the previous day's work. When the horse is to be taught any-thing which might frighten him the weather and his con-dition, both physical and mental, should be considered. If there is any doubt about going on to a new stage it is best to spend another day on work with which he is familiar.

Most horses do not have great intelligence but all have extraordinarily good memories. It is essential that the trainer should be patient in explaining to the horse what is required, taking care not to punish him for disobedience when it is caused by his not having understood what is required. If the horse is reprimanded for not understanding he will only become more frightened and confused, be made irritable and perhaps lose his temper. The trainer has to recognize the difference between a horse who is confused by the question which is being asked and the animal who is deliberately refusing to do what he fully understands is required of him. Always, the trainer must use his superior intelligence to counteract the horse's superior strength and avoid dramas and battles as much as possible.

It is often a help if the trainer rubs an aromatic oil into his hands. The presumed purpose of this is to neutralize any smell of adrenalin which the horse is quick to recognize. If he associates his trainer with an agreeable odour, progress will be made more rapidly and a greater confidence is built up between pupil and trainer. The author has discovered that any expensive scent proves satisfactory, particularly with male horses!

The essentials for training are (a) A suitable place for putting to and driving the young horse; (b) unlimited time; (c) patience; (d) an understanding of horse psychology or the willingness to acquire the same; (e) a strong set of harness, a cavesson, a lunge rein and a lunge whip; (f) a two-wheeled vehicle; (g) an assistant available for occasional help.

If the animal to be trained is well-grown and strong as a two-year-old it is advisable to spend a short time educating him gently at this age. His excellent memory will allow him to return to work as a three-year-old with a good idea of what is going to be required of him. This instils confidence and results in a bold horse. It also avoids the violence which can arise with a headstrong, unhandled three-year-old in the early training period.

Assuming that the two-year-old has been well handled and halter-broken so that he can be led about, his early lessons consist of learning to go in a large circle in both directions on the lunge rein. The purpose is to teach obedience and balance. It is a help if the private driving horse can be ridden, and it is best to accustom him to carrying someone on his back at an early age. Faults in harness work can often be corrected by a rider who, by using his legs and seat, can

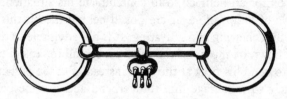

Fig. 31 Mouthing bit

place the horse into the desired position. Many enthusiasts keep one animal to serve as a hunter, hack and eventer as well as harness horse and there is no reason why one well-trained animal should not adapt himself to do all these things well. But, whatever his future may be, the early basic training of the horse is the same.

The young horse is best kept stabled during his early training and if he is visited frequently and well handled in this environment it will help him to gain confidence in his trainer.

At this stage he must be taught to accept a bridle and a simple straight bar mouthing bit (Fig. 31). Sometimes a jointed mouthing bit is used, but the disadvantage here is that the horse may learn to draw back his tongue and bring it down over the bit; this is a bad habit and one most difficult to cure.

The young horse must also get used to a roller, but be

careful that this is put on gently and not buckled up too tightly. Too tight a roller can cause a horse to arch his back like a bow, brace his front legs in resistance at the unaccustomed restriction round his middle and throw himself down in his struggles. Once a horse has been frightened in this way it will take him a very long time to get over it – if, in fact, he ever does.

Wearing his bridle and roller the horse can be left loose in his box for an hour or so to contemplate his situation. If a couple of lumps of sugar are poked behind the bit this will start him chewing and salivating. It is not advisable to tie his head down by means of the roller; it can all too easily cause him to bend his neck at the crest instead of at the poll and it is likely to encourage him to overbend and become behind his bit. It is a mistake to attempt to position the head by force at this or any other stage.

The head will come naturally enough into its place when the horse learns to go forward with his hind legs well engaged beneath his body and a correspondingly lightened forehand.

When the horse is to be taken out and worked, it is advisable to put brushing boots on all his legs to protect them against injury. Splints are often caused by a blow from the opposite hoof, and for this reason it is best to leave the young horse unshod if possible. During the early stages of lungeing the bridle and roller are removed and the horse is worked in a breaking cavesson with the tubular web lunge rein fastened to the nose ring. A cavesson used in this way gives maximum control, which would not be the case were the horse to be lunged from a headcollar. It is not advisable to lunge from the bit lest the mouth be damaged.

A long lungeing whip of the nylon variety completes the equipment needed and is essential if the work is to be carried out effectively.

The lunge rein is held in the left hand and should not be wrapped round the fingers in case the horse should jerk away. The whip is held in the right hand and pointed downwards. Before taking the horse into the school for the first time it is a help if he can be introduced to the lunge routine in a large loose-box, bedded with deep straw. He is then led round the box anti-clockwise, and the trainer should be able gradually to lengthen the lunge until he is standing in the middle of the box. The whip is held towards the quarters throughout. The horse is, in effect, now being lunged to the left without any fuss, and he should be made much of so that he realizes that his trainer is pleased. As soon as he fully understands that he is circling and going forward from the whip he should be stopped. If he is kept going to the left for too long it will be hard to persuade him to go the opposite way.

To lunge to the right the position of rein and whip are reversed and the same procedure is carried out again. It is usually far more difficult, however, to get a young horse to circle to the right and requires greater skill in the part of the trainer. Unfortunately, most people always approach and lead their foals and yearlings from the near side, but any horse which has been handled equally on the offside from birth is as easy to lunge clockwise as anti-clockwise. If the horse should refuse to go to the right the trainer can position himself just behind the line of the girth and send him forward by using the whip behind him, but without hitting the horse. At the same time, the head should be bent to the right with the lunge rein. Provided that he can be made to go forward, he will soon give in and go clockwise. Whatever happens, the trainer must not become impatient. If he does, the horse will get flustered and may lose his temper. He may then associate lungeing to the right with punishment and become even more bewildered by what is required. It usually only takes about ten minutes to get the horse walking round on the lunge in both directions in a loose box.

The pupil can now be taken to the place where he will be trained. The ideal situation is an indoor school, but if this is not available, an enclosed outside manege will do. Failing this, a makeshift school can be set up in the corner of a field, advantage being taken of existing hedges or post and rail fences to form two sides of the arena. Barbed wire fences must be avoided at all costs. It is just too easy for a frightened young horse to run straight through one. The third and fourth sides can be built, for instance, by placing jump poles on top of five gallon oil drums. Although this barricade is only about 18 inches high, it is enough to restrict the pupil if he is being troublesome and it will be helpful if he tries to nap, or hang, towards the field gate or stable.

The pupil should first be led anti-clockwise round the school, the trainer gradually lengthening the lunge rein and telling him to walk on. To send the horse forward it will be necessary to show him the whip held in the right hand. Should he, in response to this signal, rush off, however, he must not be checked but must be permitted to continue his forward movement by the lunge rein being lengthened until only one loop is left in the hand. It is necessary to retain one loop lest a sudden movement should pull the rein out of the hand. A triangle is formed by the rein, the horse, and the whip, and the trainer should stand in a line well behind the withers so that he is in a good position to keep the horse going forward. If he gets in front of the horse the pupil's reaction will be to stop and face his trainer. He may even come in to the centre of the circle, which must not be allowed. The trainer should watch the horse's eye and ears. A newcomer to lungeing may become dizzy; this is caused by watching the legs. Talk to the horse all the time and always

74

use the same words of command, said in exactly the same way. Horses learn by constant repetition.

It is a mistake to give a command which is unlikely to be obeyed as it only teaches disobedience. If the young horse tears off at a canter when he is first sent off on the circle it is quite useless to tell him to walk, it is much better to keep saying 'steady' in a calming voice until he slows down. When he is about to come to a trot the trainer can say 'trot' and he will be obeyed without any trouble because the horse was about to trot anyway. After a few trotting circles he should be sent forward into canter again and then told to trot when the moment seems appropriate. If difficulty is experienced in bringing the horse from trot or walk to halt the hedge can be used. As the pupil circles towards it the trainer steps to the front barring the way. At the same time, he says 'halt' and the horse is compelled to stop, facing the hedge. The trainer should immediately drop his whip and go to the horse to reward him, before sending him off again on the same circle with the command 'walk on'. This can be repeated several times until he associates the word 'halt' with stopping and a titbit and 'walk on' with going forward. The horse should not be encouraged to come to his trainer at any time during lungeing. He must learn to halt on the circle and stand still by himself. This is the beginning of learning to stand unheld. If he is ever allowed to turn in towards his trainer he will later use this as a resistance. The horse must be made to circle to the right as well as to the left during his first lesson, the same methods being used as when he was taught to go on the left rein. Any lack of concentration on the part of the trainer will probably result in the horse stopping and turning inwards or he may even attempt to dash off to the left. If he does, he must be stopped immediately and sent to the right and kept working until he is going calmly. The first lesson will long remain in the young horse's memory so it is essential to be firm and patient. At this stage the pupil should be beginning to gain confidence and, also, be aware that the trainer is the boss.

After the lesson the horse is put back in his box and his head collar is put on. The lunge rein can then be buckled to the back dee and passed through the tethering ring on the wall. This ring should be at least 5 feet from the ground. The trainer can hold the lunge as he rubs the horse down and gradually the horse learns to stand tied up. At this stage, should he pull back the rein will run through the ring. He can then be brought forward again by a pull on the lunge and a little encouragement from behind. He will soon find that there is little object in pulling back.

As soon as the pupil is reasonably obedient at all paces on the lungeing rein in both directions, the work can be repeated wearing the roller. If he humps his back and bucks he must be sent forward. He will calm down soon enough.

When he accepts working in a roller, a driving saddle and crupper can be put on. The crupper dock should be very soft and it should be large enough for comfort. It is a good idea to sew a piece of sheepskin round the dock part to prevent chafing. The horse can be left for an hour in the stable to get used to the feeling of the crupper. At the same time a thin rope can be tied on to the mouthing bit and passed through the terrets before being secured to the bit ring on the other side. This should only be tight enough to prevent the horse from getting his head down. There must not be any contact on the mouth when he is standing still with his head to the front. The object is to teach the horse to give with his jaw in answer to the solid resistance felt if he lowers his head, but the rope is not tight enough to allow leaning or overbending.

Work on the circle will continue as before, but now wearing the driving saddle and crupper and with the bridle and mouthing bit worn with the cavesson. The rope can remain loosely attached.

Most horses object strongly to the crupper. They will clamp their tails down and try to kick it off. This is a natural reaction and it is best not to punish the pupil. He must merely be made to go forward regardless of his tactics. For this reason it is a help to have the horse obedient before the crupper is put on. It is important at this stage to get the horse working calmly at all paces. Sometimes horses will walk and trot calmly but will erupt at the canter. If this is going to happen it is best to get it over now. Otherwise, one day when he is put to a valuable vehicle something may make him canter and the result could be a smashed cart.

When the horse has accepted the crupper the breeching is put on and the back band, belly band and tugs are fixed to the harness saddle. The breeching straps can be buckled to another pair of straps on the tugs to prevent the breeching from flying up over the horse's back if he should start to kick. He should be worked at all paces, in both directions, until he is indifferent to the pressure against his quarters.

The collar, hames and traces are now put on, the latter being passed through the tugs and coiled round themselves with the breeching straps being buckled through the trace ends. These can be tightened to accustom the horse to pressure on his quarters from the breeching. As he brings his shoulder forward the collar tightens the trace, which in turn pulls on the breeching. The spare pair of straps are looped to the terrets and buckled round the hame terrets so that the collar will not slide down the neck if the horse should lower his head. A young horse is likely to become frightened by a collar crashing down on to his ears.

The work on the lungeing rein is carried out as before and

by now the horse should be calm and obedient at all paces and happy about wearing the harness. From this point the trainer will be better able to concentrate on obtaining the rhythm and cadence of the free trot, an active walk and a square halt and should make every effort to achieve them.

If the horse is being broken to ride as well as drive the morning sessions can be spent with harness and the afternoons with a riding saddle.

As soon as he accepts the roller the saddle can be put on. He should be lunged on the cavesson wearing the mouthing bit, bridle and saddle. The stirrups can be left dangling, but it is important to see that they are high enough not to bang and bruise the elbows. When he is happy about his saddle and is going calmly he is ready to be backed (ridden). A large, loose-box which is free from low beams, mangers and hay racks is essential, but no assistant is necessary. In fact, it is preferable not to have one. Very often, the assistant is more nervous than the trainer and the smell of the adrenalin released will be transmitted to the horse. See that the box is bedded with deep litter and place a straw bale about 4 feet from the wall on one side. The pupil is led into the box wearing his riding bridle with reins. The saddle is on, but without stirrups. He should be allowed to wander round on his own whilst the trainer shuts the top and bottom doors and is then led into position between the straw bale and the swall and facing another wall. The trainer then climbs on to the bale talking all the time. He holds a chunk of mane and the reins in the left hand and can caress the horse and pat the saddle with the right hand. When the moment appears to be appropriate the trainer should spring lightly and quietly on to the horse and lie with his tummy across the saddle, patting the horse with the right hand on the offside. After a few seconds he can slide off and make a terrific fuss of the horse with titbits. This is repeated several times and should be carried out every afternoon for about five minutes until the horse relaxes. When he ceases to stiffen the trainer can put his right leg over the saddle, being careful not to touch the quarters with the leg and keeping his body low. It is the sight of someone towering above him that causes most fear in the young horse. If a titbit can be given by the trainer when he is on the horse's back, this is advantageous. Gradually, the trainer can sit up and ask the horse to walk on. The two-year-old is frequently bewildered at the prospect of moving with a weight on his back but he can be uprooted by being rocked gently to one side using open rein. He should not be asked to do more than walk round the loose-box in both directions at this stage.

All of the above can take as little as three weeks but the time involved may vary considerably from one horse to another. It all depends on individual temperaments. This is as much as the horse needs to learn as a strong two-year-old or as a normally well-grown three-year-old.

Chapter 6

FURTHER TRAINING

After his early training the young horse should be turned away for a year to grow. His education will advance more favourably if he is put in a field where he can see traffic and people. He will then not feel cut off from the world of activity which he has recently known.

On the first day that he is brought up to further his education he is best lunged in a cavesson to settle him down before asking anything else of him. He will remember all that he learnt the year before and provided that he was well taught, will be obedient. He will, undoubtedly, have grown stronger and it will be a relief to his trainer that confidence and respect were attained when he was less developed.

He should now be introduced to long reins. The driving saddle, crupper, riding bridle and cavesson are put on as before, the lunge rein is buckled to the cavesson and the long reins to the bit. A Fulmer snaffle (Fig. 32) is now preferable to a mouthing bit. The cheeks prevent the bit from being pulled sideways through the mouth and the thick mouthpiece is mild. It can, in fact, be made even more so by sewing a piece of bicycle inner tubing round it if this is thought to be necessary. When the horse is circled anti-clockwise, the left long rein goes directly from the bit to the left hand alongside the lunge rein from the cavesson. The right rein is passed from the bit, behind the saddle terrets to the right hand and held with the whip. The ends of the long reins should be left unbuckled, otherwise it is easy to get a foot through the loop and be pulled over. The horse is worked on the circle under the control of the cavesson and lunge at this stage. When he is accustomed to the long rein lying over his back he can be taken for a walk round the field, the trainer walking behind

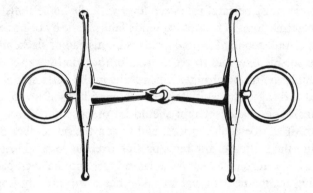

Fig. 32 Fulmer snaffle

and to one side, exerting a light feeling on the horse's mouth. Very often it will be found that the weight of the reins alone gives sufficient contact. When the pupil is no longer afraid and can be inclined to the left and right, the cavesson and lunge can be removed but the long reins are not passed through the terrets. An untrained horse is capable of wrapping himself up like a parcel if the reins are put through the terrets too soon and then the trainer is quite helpless. Also, it is very much more difficult to stop a horse on a rein which goes via a terret. The horse can now progress to being worked at all paces and be taught to change the rein. Do not attempt this at the trot, however, until the horse has learnt to turn calmly across the school at the walk. If he is going anti-clockwise, the trainer should walk to the left of the horse's nearside hip. Now, if the contact on the right rein is slackened and the tension increased on the left one the horse will turn across the school to the left. As he reaches the centre the trainer will be behind him and must then step smartly to the right, taking the reins over the horse's back. Pressure on the left rein is then released and contact taken on the right. The trainer must be careful to keep level with the horse's offside hip at this point. The most common faults made by beginners are to pull too hard on the inside rein, instead of slackening the outside one, and to get in front of the pupil towards the completion of the change. This results in the horse stopping and turning to face his trainer, wrapping himself up in the reins. The change of rein should be practised at the walk until it can be achieved with agility and the horse does not mind the feeling of the reins passing over his loins. Then it can be performed at a slow, balanced trot with an even pace being maintained throughout. The horse will quickly learn to turn when a slight feel is put on to his mouth.

The reins can now be put through the terrets. The inside rein will govern the bend and the outside control the pace. A delicate hand is needed for successful work on long reins for rough handling and misuse will soon produce a hard-mouthed or over-bent horse. Suppling exercises, such as loops, serpentines, figures-of-eight, large and small circles should be a daily routine and the horse must learn to lengthen and shorten his stride at a cadenced trot. His head should not be pulled into place by the reins. It will gradually go into the desired position when the forehand is lightened by increased hock action. As the horse becomes more athletic and better balanced it will be found that the head carriage will improve. He should not be restricted by sharp bits and check reins;

these will only make him hollow his back, trail his hocks and shorten his stride.

Once the horse is safe to long-rein in the field, he may be taken out for walks and learn to face and pass the hazards of the outside world. When he is confident and quiet in traffic, he can go on to a further stage.

The open bridle is now replaced by a winkered driving bridle fitted, for preference, with a Wilson snaffle. If the horse is inclined to open his mouth and cross his jaw, a dropped noseband can be added to the bridle but the driving noseband must remain to prevent the cheek pieces from gaping when pressure is put on to the bit. Horses usually find winkers very bewildering at first, and so it is advisable to work in them on the lunge to begin with. Wearing winkers the pupil can no longer see his trainer and has to obey solely by voice. This is where the confidence and obedience which were established during the earlier training bears fruit. The whip should *not* be used. If the horse feels, or hears, a whip coming from an unknown direction he will become a bundle of nerves and weeks of training can be undone in a few seconds. It is important to keep talking to him so that he knows that he is not alone and care must be taken to prevent him from running into any object which he could see and avoid if he was in an open bridle. For working anti-clockwise the lunge rein is buckled to the offside snaffle rings, passed over the poll and down through the nearside snaffle rings to the hand. The horse should be allowed to go round gently to accustom him to the blinding effect of winkers. When he is worked clockwise, the lunge rein must, of course, be changed so that it is buckled in opposite fashion.

As soon as the horse has lengthened his stride again and is going forward with confidence the long reins can be put on to the driving bridle. They are passed through the hame and pad terrets to the hand. The lunge rein remains in case of emergency. Going to the left, the lunge rein is held in the left hand and the long reins and whip in the right hand, contact being gradually taken up by the long reins.

When the horse is calm the lunge can be removed and all the work which was done in an open bridle is repeated in the driving bridle.

The horse should now be ready to pull a load but he must be introduced to the job slowly. Start by putting the traces through the tugs and breeching and then fix an 8-foot length of rope with a loop on the end to each trace. These loops are then attached to a swingle tree which the assistant can hold with the traces hanging slack. The lunge rein should then be buckled on to the bridle again and the trainer takes charge of both lunge and long reins. The horse is asked to walk on and when he is going freely forwards the assistant can begin to lean back slightly on the swingle tree. This must be done gently at first until the horse becomes accustomed to pressure on his collar, but as he learns to lean into his work more weight can be put on to the traces and the horse can be taken for walks along quiet lanes with either the assistant or the trainer leaning on the swingle tree.

When the horse is happy about pulling a weight, he should be accustomed to a noise behind him. If an assistant is available he can be pressed into dragging a bar with a chain on it whilst the trainer is long reining, as a start. If no help is possible, the trainer can take the pupil out on long reins and lunge and drag the sound effects himself. Should the horse become frightened he should be stopped and reassured, only being started when he has calmed down.

The horse can now progress to the horse dragging a bar or very light log (about 3 inches in diameter) along the lanes. It must, of course, be fixed well clear of the horse's heels. Roads

are preferable to tracks or rough grass for this work. On the
latter the bar is too easily caught on uneven ground and may
then drag violently on the collar, upsetting and possibly
terrorizing the pupil. It is a great mistake to ask any horse,
and particularly a well-bred one, to drag a heavy log. The
difficulty in starting, and the dead pull of moving a solid
weight is apt to frighten him and the end product may be a
jibbing horse who, when he does go forward, proceeds in a
series of kangaroo-like bounds. Once this habit is acquired it
is hard to persuade him to start even the lightest vehicle in the
approved manner of gently leaning into the collar and walking quietly.

The pupil is now ready to be introduced to the feel of
shafts and for this purpose two 8-foot garden canes are
passed through the breeching and tied with a piece of binder
twine inside the tugs. When the pupil is quite indifferent to
the presence of the canes against his sides, and can be
long-reined with them in position, the canes can be replaced
by two saplings of about 1 inch diameter. The end of the
saplings are left to drag along the ground. It is important to
see that they protrude through the tugs far enough to come
level with the hames, for if they are too short the ends may
get under the collar and therefore frighten the horse.

If these little exercises are carried out quietly there should
be no trouble when the horse is put to his first vehicle. For
the next stage the author uses a wheel-less breaking cart
(Fig. 33), designed like a cross between a conveyance such as
the Ancient Britons used and a sleigh. The construction is of
greenwood poles (elm suckers 1 to 3 inches in diameter are
suitable) nailed together and reinforced with binder twine. If
the horse takes off with a vehicle like this he can be swung in a
circle on the lunge and the contraption will just skid sideways
without turning over. Its disadvantage is that it will not go

backwards. An ordinary vehicle will have one wheel turning backwards and one forwards when a sharp turn is made, which is easier for the horse. The wheel-less cart is harder to

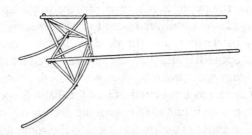

Fig. 33 Wheel-less cart

turn and requires stronger shaft pressure, but its advantages outweigh this failing.

It is, of course, more usual to use a long-shafted breaking cart. In the days when a great many horses were being broken

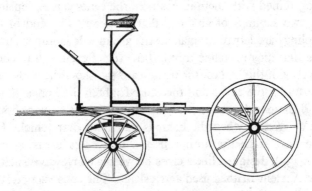

Fig. 34 Skeleton break

to harness there was not time for all the preliminaries that now take place. A young horse was just harnessed alongside a reliable old hand in a skeleton break (Fig. 34) and was forcibly restrained or dragged along by his partner until he learnt to do the job required of him.

Before the horse is put to the wheel-less cart, as a wise precaution, he should be worked on the circle in all his harness on long reins until he is thoroughly relaxed and a bit tired.

Weather conditions, most importantly, must be ideal. If there is torrential rain or a howling gale, abandon the project, until the sun shines again. The stage must be set carefully and everyone around the place should be told what is going on otherwise someone is bound to come round the corner pushing a noisy wheelbarrow just as the pupil is being put to.

Putting to a semi-trained horse must not be attempted without an assistant. A walled stable yard is an ideal situation, the cart being drawn up about 9 feet from, and facing, a wall. The horse can then be brought into the yard wearing all his harness, except the breeching, and with a lunge rein buckled on to each side of the bit. Let him sniff the contraption until he is quite calm, then bring him in front of it so that he is standing facing the wall. The trainer stands on the nearside and holds the head by the lunge rein in the left hand. The right hand is then free to guide the shaft through the tug as the assistant, who is on the other side and also holding a lunge rein, draws the vehicle quietly up to the horse, putting the shaft through the right tug. The traces can be quickly tied on with string using a quick-release knot, whilst the trainer holds the horse still, then the belly band is buckled. There is no need to use breeching; it is only one more thing to have to unfasten in an emergency.

It is absolutely imperative that the horse be put to quickly and quietly and to this end every move should be planned in advance. In this way the pupil will not be frightened by some careless action. Although having the horse facing a wall helps

87

with putting to it makes moving off more difficult because the horse has to start by turning. To help the horse execute this manoeuvre the trainer pulls the left shaft towards him with his right hand as the command to walk on is given, by bringing the horse to the left with his hand whilst the assistant pushes on the right shaft. The horse is then walked in a circle to the left with the shafts being pushed and pulled as necessary. The trainer should talk and reassure the pupil all the time, and if he gets frightened the work must stop and the horse be given time to relax before going on again. If possible, he should be taken round on the right circle as well. When he has gone quietly for a few minutes he can be stopped facing the wall where he was put to. Equal care must be taken in getting him out of the vehicle. It is probably best accomplished if the trainer holds the horse whilst the assistant unfastens the belly band and traces and lifts the cart back and well clear of the horse's quarters.

The exercise should be repeated once or twice a day until the horse is no longer afraid. He can then be taken for walks along the lanes in his cart on long reins, but the lunge should remain buckled as a precaution.

Now the horse is ready to be put to a wheeled cart, but it is important that the vehicle should be a two-wheeler. If the horse suddenly turns round with this sort of cart it will follow him whereas, in similar circumstances, a four-wheeled vehicle will articulate and probably turn over. The same precautions that applied to putting to the wheel-less cart apply to the wheeled one, only this time the breeching must be buckled and it is best to have a kicking strap. This can be improvised by securing a webbing halter to the offside shaft level with the loins.

Once the horse is put to, the rope is passed over his loins, through the back piece of the crupper and tied on to the nearside shaft in a quick release knot. Its purpose is to discourage kicking but it should not be tied down too tightly or it may have the opposite effect should the horse canter. The procedure for starting and leading is the same as it was for the wheel-less cart and, as before, both trainer and assistant should have lungeing reins.

The horse will probably find the new sensation somewhat bewildering. His vehicle now rolls instead of drags and there is no vibration and no noise. Nevertheless, after a few circuits of the stable yard in both directions, he will probably be ready to go out on to the road. If all is well, the assistant can remove the right lunge rein and take the left one, whilst the trainer can walk alongside the saddle on the nearside, holding the driving reins. When the horse appears to be calm, it is time for the trainer to mount the vehicle. This is best done in motion for the reason that if the pupil is asked to pull a vehicle from a halt on the first occasion it is loaded the unaccustomed weight may cause him to jib. Gradually, the assistant can drop back behind the winkers and once the horse is going calmly can remove the lunge rein.

When this stage has been reached, the horse should be driven gently every day along quiet roads with flat surfaces. Until he is absolutely steady he should be lunged before being put to each day. Eventually the young horse has to be taught to stand unheld during and after putting to. Any tendency to rush off at these times must be checked calmly by the trainer. There is no need to hit the horse or jab him in the mouth. Very often, indeed, a young horse who has been fussing suddenly stands quite still and gives a resigned sigh. When he does so he should immediately be patted and rewarded. He will soon learn to stand in anticipation of his titbit.

During the early stages it is important to ensure that the

neck and shoulder muscles are not made to ache by taking the pupil too far or by overloading the vehicle.

The first and last half miles should always be driven at the walk so that he does not learn to rush away from, or towards his stable. Hill work must be introduced gradually. Steep, downhill gradients are best avoided until the pupil has learnt how to hold the vehicle back with his breeching on slight slopes and through decreasing transitions of pace. It can be terrifying for a young horse to be pushed down a hill by his vehicle; he feels that his hind legs are going from under him and he can very easily become so frightened that he is spoilt for harness work for ever. Equally, steep uphill work may make him collar-shy if he finds that he cannot pull the cart without his shoulders being hurt. Once his muscles have developed, uphill work can be gradually introduced and increased.

At every opportunity the young horse should be taken out in company. One other horse and vehicle is enough, at first, to introduce him to the sights and sounds which he will meet in the future. To start with, he should be driven behind the other turn-out so that he can see it; then he can be driven in front and finally alongside. The sound of a turn-out upsides with him, which he cannot see, is another frightening matter for the young horse and it is preferable to accustom him to it at home rather than at a show where there is so much else to bewilder him.

It is not advisable to teach the horse to back until he is fairly advanced in his education, otherwise he may use it as an evasion. Backing is easily taught by standing in front of, and facing, the horse. One hand pushes the nose and the other the chest at the command 'get back'. If the horse does not move, the trainer can tread on a hoof. As soon as the horse takes one step back he should be rewarded and led forward.

The procedure is repeated until three or four steps are achieved. He should be brought forward again each time before he is rewarded. Quite quickly he will learn to step back when his mouth is felt and he hears the command.

When the young horse is quiet to drive, it is only necessary to drive him about three times a week. His other working days can be spent on long reins in an open bridle and driving saddle to improve his paces and head carriage. The advantages of continuing the long rein training are that the trainer can see exactly where the horse is placing his feet and how he is carrying his head, neither of which can be properly seen from a vehicle. The horse should not be over-schooled; the object is to produce a free-moving, quiet and contented horse.

If the horse was backed (ridden) in his early training, and is to be ridden in the future, his riding education should progress concurrently with the driving work just described.

On the first day that he is to be ridden he should be well lunged in a riding saddle, open bridle and cavesson before being mounted in a loose-box. If all goes well he should be ridden round the box before being taken outside. It is not advisable to take him out into a large open field until he has been ridden at all paces in a small enclosure. A grassy stock-yard is ideal if an indoor school is not available, but otherwise an enclosed outdoor ring is satisfactory. When he can be safely ridden he should be taken out for gentle hacks alongside a traffic-proof and sensible schoolmaster.

If the youngster's work is divided between driving, riding and long reining, his interest will be maintained and the result will be a happy horse.

Chapter 7

SHOWING CONSIDERED

When the horse is four years old his first public outing in harness can be considered. He should, by now, be quiet to drive both alone and in company and be sensible in traffic. He will have been taught to load into a box or trailer without fuss, and should have been taken for a few short journeys to accustom him to travelling. If a radio has been regularly left on within earshot of his stable the sounds of music and strange voices over a loudspeaker are not likely to hold any terrors for him.

The complications with which the private driving exhibitor is faced in assembling all that constitutes a turn-out are considerable. He has to produce a well-mannered horse, a suitable vehicle, a set of show harness, a pair of lamps, a whip, an apron and the means of transport to convey all these items to a chosen destination. Getting the well-appointed turn-out to its first show can become a challenge.

Apart from the horse, the vehicle is the most important item. It is essential that it be suitable for the animal concerned. If the horse is a sporty, robust type, such as a Welsh cob, then he would look well in a sporting vehicle like a dog cart, but it would be a mistake to put such a workmanlike cob to a Park Phaeton, the elegance of which calls for a lighter type of horse.

The Vehicle. The increasing interest in driving is making vehicles hard to locate. A hundred years ago a new carriage could be ordered from the village coachbuilder and the ideas and whims of the individual purchaser would be painstakingly carried out. Further, second hand vehicles were plentiful and were regularly advertised in the newspaper columns.

Nowadays, finding a suitable vehicle can be an exhausting occupation. A few still remain undiscovered in the out-houses and coach-houses of large country estates; farm auctions and house sales occasionally produce a vehicle but usually the number of buyers far exceed the available carriages. Sales of interest to the driving enthusiast are regularly held at Reading, however, and an advertisement in the British Driving Society's Newsletter may prove fruitful.

A vehicle unearthed from the back of a barn should be meticulously examined before being purchased. The most important question is whether it will fit the horse concerned. The shafts should be held at draught height and the distance from the tug stop to the ground measured. This is a measurement which should have been previously taken with the horse in harness, when the tugs were buckled to the central holes of the back band. The length and width of the shafts should also be measured. Some vehicles have fittings which enable the shafts to be altered for height, length and width to accommodate various horses and tug stops are frequently adjustable, giving a choice of three fittings. Body height can be altered up to about four inches by adding (or removing the existing) blocks of wood between the axle and springs. A check should be made, also, to ensure that the wheels are a pair. Sometimes, one tyre is put on too tightly, causing a wheel to become overdished. This defect can best be seen when the vehicle is viewed from behind. Spokes and felloes should be examined for looseness, rot and excessive wood worm. Very often, the part of the felloe which has rested on an earth floor for years will have become soggy and rotted away. Loose spokes and damaged felloes can result in an expensive visit to the wheelwright but wood worm, in small quantities, is of little consequence. It can be effectively treated and exterminated with wood worm killer. If the vehicle is rubber-shod note should be taken of the condition of the rubbers. If they are badly worn, the channels may have been damaged and where they are wired on (as opposed to the clencher type) some difficulty may be experienced in replacing them. In either of these two cases both the channels and the rubbers would have to be renewed, adding considerable cost to the vehicle. The body should be examined for rot, wood worm and cracks.

Unless a vehicle is purchased in show condition it will need to be restored before being taken into the show ring. The standard of turn-out in private driving classes has risen so rapidly during the past twelve years. An unrestored vehicle would be a great disadvantage.

The newcomer to driving should beware of a recently, but badly, painted vehicle. One thick coat of paint and some inadequate lining may perhaps have been applied, but it is possible that this will be hiding from the inexperienced eye a multitude of imperfections. Putty or fibre glass compound, for instance, can be used as a temporary filling for large areas of otherwise non-existent felloes and hubs. It is much safer to buy a completely unrestored vehicle and have it restored properly than to take on one of the putty and paint types.

An expertly restored vehicle is almost certain to be sound. No craftsman would dream of spending hours painting over rotten surfaces.

Show Harness. Harness for showing looks smartest if it is made from black leather with brass or silver-plated furniture. If the vehicle has brass fittings, the harness should have brass mounts to match. The outside surfaces of the winkers, collar, pad, or driving saddle, and false martingale front should be of patent leather and there should be no colour trimmings – these are reserved for trade turn-outs. The rest of the harness is of black leather. The lining of the collar may be made with either black or brown leather. Traces, back band, belly band, girth straps, back strap, loin strap, breeching straps are all made of two layers of leather stitched together with two or four rows of stitching. On some cheaper harness a machine will have been run along the surface of single straps leaving a row of stitching holes to give the appearance of stitched double leather, but a close scrutiny will easily detect this. Buckles throughout the harness should match in shape. A little distinction can be achieved by the employment of discreet crests or monograms worn on the centre of the winkers, rosettes, false martingale and either side of the pad or saddle below the terrets. It is usual to have tan reins with black harness. Black ones would leave a disagreeable dye on the gloves and apron.

If the vehicle is of a country type and made with varnished wood, brown harness is most suitable.

Lamps. The metal trim round the lamps should, to be correct, match the furniture of the harness and fittings of the vehicle, i.e. brass furniture should be accompanied by brass-mounted lamps. The lamps themselves must be businesslike and unfussy; those enormous affairs with ornate tops are not really suitable for private driving. The square or oval-fronted and square-sided lamps are much better (see Figs

35–37). A small rear lamp can also be carried as in Fig. 38. For the show ring new candles, which have been lighted and immediately blown out, are fitted in the lamps. The idea is that on a windy night, with only two matches available,

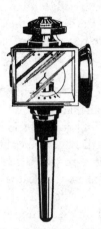

Fig. 35 Side view of oval-fronted lamp

Fig. 36 Front view of same lamp

Fig. 37 Square lamp

Fig. 38 Rear lamp

a candle which has already been lit will light more readily. It is never correct for flowers to take the place of candles inside lamps.

In some private stables, in the old days, lamps were not put on to vehicles before 3 p.m. If they were carried on the carriage in daylight they were reversed so that the glass side faced towards the vehicle to protect the side glasses from mud until they were required. Nowadays it is usual to carry lamps in the working position on show vehicles regardless of the time of day or the condition of the mud. To reflect the light the insides of lamps are frequently silver-plated on copper.

The whip should be of a suitable size for the horse and vehicle. A full-size whip would be cumbersome with a pony turn-out.

The apron, or knee rug, should blend with the colours of the vehicle and upholstery. Fawn shows less dirt and hairs than a dark colour on which grey hairs show badly. Bright colours are again a mistake.

Dress. The dress of the Whip is important and the main considerations are neatness and practicability. For lady Whips, tight skirts and high-heeled shoes are best avoided. Rubber-soled shoes are preferable as they do not scratch the paint, and for the rest a coat and skirt and small-brimmed hat does very well. Hats with wide brims are disastrous. A high wind, a pulling horse and a salute to the Royal Box can become a nightmare in such creations. Gentleman Whips wear suits and bowler hats. The fit of the gloves requires some attention. Those which are a size too large will be found to be more comfortable for driving and they are best made from soft unlined leather of medium weight. It is a good idea to carry a spare pair of wool or string gloves under the seat cushion in case of rain. If the Whip wishes to wear a button-hole, the yellow carnation, which is the flower of the British Driving Society, adds a discreet touch of colour.

A leather boot-lace and a sharp penknife makes a useful repair kit for emergencies and should be carried at all times.

Transport. Transporting a turn-out can be a problem. The easiest method, undoubtedly, is to use a horsebox, when the whole unit can be loaded without trouble. Other methods involve two drivers, one with a car and vehicle trailer and the second with a Land-Rover and horse trailer. Costs are then doubled unnecessarily and it may not always be possible to find a helper who is able to drive. The system used by the author, which only requires one driver, is for the vehicle to be carried in an open-backed Land-Rover, easily adapted to this purpose, and the horse trailer just hitched on behind in the usual way. A simple hand-operated winch is fitted between the driver and passenger seats to work the block and tackle, by means of which the vehicle is drawn up two narrow ramps (carried on bolts on the side of the trailer when they are not in use) and into the body of the Land-Rover. Once in position the carriage wheels rest on wooden blocks fitted on the back seats over the rear wheels of the Land-Rover and the shafts lie on top of the cab pointing over the bonnet. The vehicle is secured by the winch, and shafts and wheels are tied with ropes.

Chapter 8

PREPARING FOR AND GOING TO A SHOW

The first appearance in public will leave an indelible impression on the young horse's memory. It is important that he should not be alarmed by his experiences on this occasion and therefore the first public outing must be chosen with care. Try to find a show where there is an adequate exercising area and a large flat ring, rather than one held on a small ground with a tiny ring on the side of a hill. The classification laid out in the schedule should then be studied thoroughly. The wording is likely to read something like this.

Private Driving Class. Stallion, mare or gelding, any height, to be shown in single or double harness to a suitable vehicle. Show waggons and commercial vehicles are excluded. Excessive speed is not required and the suitability of exhibits for private driving purposes will be specially considered.

SECTION A Non-Hackney Type, Single Harness 14 h.h. and under.

SECTION B Non-Hackney Type, Single Harness over 14 h.h.

SECTION C Hackney Type Single Harness

SECTION D Hackney and Non-Hackney Type, Pairs and Tandems.

A 'Showing Class' as just described, in which no marathon
is involved, is preferable for introducing the young horse
gently to the show ring. The possible bustle of a seven-mile
drive on the roads with horses behind, in front and passing
may bother the youngster at first and, if he hots up, it may
be difficult to settle him. Once he has been to a couple of
shows without marathons and emerged unworried, he can be
taken to a show which has a marathon drive. It is unlikely
that he will then get excited. Some experienced horses will
look forward to going on the drive after a few preliminary
circuits of the ring have been completed and are clearly
disappointed if they are taken back to their horseboxes
instead of out on to the road. A show which has a marathon
will state clearly on the schedule that exhibitors will be
required to complete a drive of . . . . miles (usually between
five and seven) before returning to the ring for final judging.
The time allowed for the drive gives an average speed of
about seven miles an hour, which is little more than a hound
jog.

As soon as the entry has been sent in, serious preparation
should commence. The young horse must be driven daily.
Normally he may be taken out in working harness and an
exercising vehicle but now he should be driven in his show-
vehicle and show-harness a few times to make sure that he
goes quietly in them and that everything fits properly. His
show-collar must be worn frequently to ensure that it will
not rub when he wears it at the show. If it has been made to
measure it will, in any case, need to be worn and broken in
before it will settle comfortably on to his shoulders.

For exhibitors who are without help, the show preparations
are less arduous if they are spread over four days. Heels,
mane, tail and jawline can be trimmed as applicable. Moun-
tain and moorland breeds are frequently shown untrimmed

and unplaited, but this is largely a matter for personal choice and may also depend upon whether the animal is to be shown in any other capacity, such as in-hand classes when full manes, tails and feather are required.

The vehicle can be prepared on the third day as described in Chapter 10.

Harness cleaning can occupy the second day. It has to be shiny as well as supple when it appears in the show ring and if it is to be cleaned thoroughly it should be taken entirely to pieces. A set of single harness can be reduced to thirty-six parts. All the surfaces should be wiped with a damp cloth which has been wrung out in tepid water. On no account should any leather be left to soak in water. Excess water removes all the oils from the hide resulting in dried-out and cracked leather. Saddle soap needs to be rubbed well into the reins and all the inside leather surfaces. Outside surfaces (unless patent) should be brushed with black boot polish. Patent areas can be cleaned with patent cleaner. Metal polish is applied sparingly to the metal parts, taking care not to get the polish on to the leather. Leather protectors, made of thin metal, used to be available with a shaped hole cut to fit over the crest to protect surrounding leather from metal polish during cleaning. The leather which has been covered in shoe polish should now be brushed until it shines and then it can be finished with a soft cloth. The patent parts will need a rub and finally the metal is polished.

The harness is assembled before being put into soft cloth bags and should then be stored in its travelling trunk and left in a dry place so that the metal will not tarnish. Material with a rough weave should be avoided as wrapping as the harsh threads may leave indentations on the patent if any pressure is applied from the weight of the harness.

Harness should normally be hung on racks in a dry room.

Moth and wood worm must be guarded against as both will attack leather which is left dirty and neglected in a box. Moth grubs eat stitching and leather and wood worm delight in collars, cruppers and saddles. Harness which is put away for the winter should be stripped, thoroughly greased and hung up in as many separate pieces as possible with buckles left undone lest the steel tongues corrode and rot the leather. Patent parts, of course, should not be greased. The set is best covered with a light cloth to protect it from dust and ideally a glass-fronted harness case is the best storage place—unfortunately such refinements are not easily found today.

Lamps cleaned and wrapped in cloths can be packed into a box ready for travelling.

If the horse needs to be reshod, this should be attended to two days before the show. The shoes will then have time to settle. Exceptionally heavy shoes are not necessary for private driving classes. A fullered out, concave, hunter shoe is ideal. Calkins on the outside heels of the hind shoes with a compensating feather-edged wedge heel on the inside are advantageous for some horses, but this is purely a matter for individual opinion. Some exhibitors favour the use of Mordax studs.

Feeding, affecting the show-day performance, should start two days before the show. The fat and muscle which constitute show condition will have been built up gradually throughout the past two years, but the protein intake during the last forty-eight hours needs careful regulation in some cases. The quietest animal may become wildly excited at his first public outing and a surfeit of oats will not help. If the horse is likely to hot up it may be wise to reduce his corn ration before his first show and replace it with chopped carrots, apples and extra bulk. Cutting down the corn on the morning of the show will have little effect on his performance a few hours later if he has been corned-up during the preceding days.

On the morning of the day before the show the young horse should be taken for his usual drive and kept out for at least two hours. In the afternoon, his white socks, if he has them, and mane and tail can be scrubbed in warm water and soapless shampoo. If he is a grey and the weather is warm he can be given a bath in warm water, but be careful to dry him really well. Woollen stable bandages put on his legs over Gamgee tissue will keep them warm and clean. These can remain on overnight and will be ready for travelling the next morning. He should be lunged immediately after his washing to get his circulation going. It is very dangerous to bath a horse if the weather is cold or windy and unless he can be dried quickly. If ordinary soap is used, care should be taken to remove all traces during rinsing, otherwise the horse will become sticky and itchy. Detergents should never be used as they remove natural oils too readily. A clean summer sheet put on under the night rug will keep the horse free from any grease which might be picked up from the lining of the latter.

The vehicle should, if possible, be loaded ready for travelling on the day before the show to avoid a last-minute rush and a possible accident.

On the show morning there will be little to do. The horse should be fed and left in peace to eat whilst his owner is having breakfast. He is then groomed and plaited and knee pads and tail bandage put on for travelling. An anti-sweat string rug can then be put under the day rug or summer sheet and the horse is ready to box.

It is essential to allow plenty of time for travelling so that the young horse does not get upset by a rough journey and hasty handling. An unhurried and unagitated owner is likely to produce a calm horse. An adrenalin-packed exhibitor will produce a neurotic animal.

On arrival at the showground the horse should be unloaded and ridden around on a loose rein at the walk for about an hour. He should then be allowed to stand and watch anything which interests or frightens him. If he is known to be afraid of pigs it is advisable to keep well away from their pens, so that he is not unnecessarily upset on his first outing. After an hour's walking he can be worked at all paces for another hour or so and can then be returned to his box and given a feed.

He should be prepared, harnessed and put to so that he is ready about half an hour before he is due to appear in the collecting ring, and then walked and trotted about quietly in his vehicle to allow him to settle.

It is a good plan, in a crowded collecting ring, to follow a quiet animal who obviously knows his job. Nappy or fiery-looking horses are best given a wide berth. They may have a bad psychological effect on the young horse. He will be susceptible to atmosphere and the influence of a badly behaved horse may make him think that there is something to worry about.

When the class is called into the ring, allow plenty of room between the young horse and the turn-out in front. This will give him space to stride on, if he wishes to do so. It is a pity to restrict him unnecessarily and the judge will get more chance to see the turn-out if it is out on its own rather than in a crowd. It is a great mistake to get into a huddle and drive round the ring three abreast. Not only do the horses become upset but the judge is denied a clear view of the individual turn-outs. The young horse should not be hurried or asked to give a spectacular performance. A quiet, steady pace is all that is required on this first occasion. If he is asked to extend before he has settled, he will either run or get flustered and canter, and this may result in similar disappointing performances in the future. Be content with a well-mannered presentation; more noteworthy exhibitions will follow during the coming weeks.

Turn-outs are usually asked to go round the ring in a clockwise direction but the steward may then direct exhibitors to change the rein and go anti-clockwise.

The judge will be watching for the qualities of courage and presence in his winner. A free-moving, long-striding horse, covering the ground with little apparent effort and looking sensible enough to be a pleasant drive, is the one that will catch his eye. He must, in addition, be of a true harness type and be put to a vehicle which compliments him.

After a few circuits of the ring the turn-outs will be called in and lined up to face the grandstand and the judge will begin his inspection. The general conformation of the horse will be regarded most particularly. A good harness horse will have strong quarters and hind legs, be deep through the heart and have adequate breadth across the chest. The shoulder can be straighter than is permitted in a riding horse, but sound, strong limbs, which are free from blemishes likely to cause unsoundness, are essential. Perhaps most important of all are well-shaped feet with no tendency towards contracted heels. A small head and good length of rein give an attractive appearance. (Incidentally, a collar looks much better on a long neck than on a short one.) Such a horse is likely to be pleasant to drive. One with a coarse head and bull neck may lean or pull.

The harness will be inspected for fit and cleanliness and the vehicle examined for fit, soundness, balance, condition of the paint and, again, for cleanliness.

Accessories, like the whip, lamps and apron are taken into

consideration and the Whip's dress will not pass unnoticed.

When all the turn-outs have been carefully looked at, each one may be asked to go out to give an individual show. This amounts to walking quietly out of line, trotting up in front of the stands and turning in a half circle, at the same cadence, before trotting back past the stands. The horse can be made to halt and rein back four paces. He should then be taken behind the others and brought forward into his place in line. During the individual show, the judge will be looking for any tendency towards collar shyness or nappiness as the horse is asked to leave the others. He will then watch for dishing, plaiting or moving wide behind as the horse is trotted away from and towards him. Calmness and obedience will be considered.

The judge may drive some of the turn-outs before reaching his final conclusion.

Finally, rosettes and prizes will be awarded. Do remember that whatever decision the judge has made must be accepted with a smile. No exhibitor should ever query the judge's decision or show disappointment at not having been placed higher. Showing in harness is fun and will only remain so as long as exhibitors compete in the right spirit.

After the class, the horse should be taken back to the box, unharnessed, cooled off and loaded. He can be watered, fed and bandaged ready for travelling.

It is advantageous to take the young horse to another show within a few days and follow a similar routine.

Providing that he remains quiet, he can soon be taken to a show with a marathon, when he should follow a reliable horse on the drive, driven by an experienced Whip who will not rush down hills nor stop halfway up them. Both these examples of bad driving are distressing to young horses.

The more shows and rallies that the horse goes to, the

quieter he will become and gradually more can be asked of him. He will learn to extend when he goes up the grandstand side of the ring and, as he becomes better balanced and more experienced, he will be able to produce a spectacular show when asked for one by his Whip.

When he is really calm he can be taken in for driving competitions and it is then that the early months of schooling will probably be rewarded with a quiet, clear round.

Chapter 9

VEHICLES FOR PRIVATE DRIVING

The huge variety of vehicles suitable for private driving can mostly be divided into five groups: Phaetons, Gigs, Dog Carts and their offshoots, Governess Carts and the larger carriages such as Breaks and Drags. The Curricle, Cabriolet and Cocking Cart are individual vehicles, and unfortunately few examples survive.

Carriages such as Broughams, Landaus and Victorias are essentially coachman-driven vehicles and for this reason are not suitable for showing in private driving classes.

A group of vehicles which were collectively known as Phaetons began to appear in the late 1700s and progressed throughout the subsequent century.

The name Phaeton was first used in the late eighteenth century and is said to have originated from classical Greek mythology. Phaeton, who was the son of Helios, the sun god, was anxious to drive his father's sun chariot. His attempts nearly ended in disaster when the horses got away with him, almost setting fire to the earth before they were stopped.

Phaetons were designed in many different shapes and sizes for singles, pairs and, in a few cases, teams. They all had three features in common which together distinguished them from other vehicles. They were open carriages suitable for the owner to drive for pleasure. All had four wheels. All were driven from a forward-facing seat built to accommodate the Whip and a passenger. Elegant Phaetons with graceful curves were built for ladies to drive. Vehicles on more robust lines were made for gentleman Whips. Fashionable carriages were designed for town driving, whilst Phaetons with basket-work bodies were favoured for taking children out in the country. These required less maintenance than coach-painted bodies, which easily became scratched and chipped.

The earliest Phaeton was the Highflyer. This was an extremely high vehicle, but reports of one with 8-feet high rear wheels were probably an over-estimate caused by a contemporary artist overstating the size on canvas in order to paint a more spectacular picture. The young bloods, nevertheless, were said to have serenaded their ladies on first-floor balconies from the seats of their Highflyers.

The name Highflyer referred to Perch High Phaetons and Crane Neck Phaetons. The Perch High Phaeton was built on a straight wooden perch offering a limited lock. The Crane Neck Phaeton was constructed on two iron perches. These were bent in such a way as to permit the front wheels to turn under the arches giving a full lock, which made the vehicle more manœuvrable in the narrow streets of the towns. There is a fine example of the Crane Neck Phaeton in the Science Museum in London.

The Prince of Wales (later King George IV), followed by his young sporting friends, made the sport of Highflyer-driving very fashionable. They were frequently seen at race meetings and in the Park and a number of matches were run with teams put to these dangerously high vehicles.

W. B. Adams, the coachbuilder, is reported to have said of the Highflyer: 'To sit on such a seat when the horses were going at much speed would require as much skill as is evinced by a rope-dancer at a theatre. None but an extremely robust constitution could stand the violent jolting of such a vehicle over the stones of a paved road.'

Some early Phaetons were fitted with a safety device which was controlled from the driving seat and connected to the pole head. This was invented to enable the leaders, when postillion-driven, to be released, complete with bars and traces, in times of stress (such as a postillion rider losing control or falling off, when the coachman would be powerless to control the wheelers).

About thirty years later, in 1824, George IV required a vehicle which would afford more safety and easier access than the Highflyer, and so a little Phaeton, suitable for a pair of ponies, was designed. It had small wheels and was entered by a low step whilst the lines of the body and splashboards were gracefully curved. The dash was high and bent very slightly towards the horses' quarters.

Four years later, Princess Victoria had a pony Phaeton built to a similar specification. A team of four ponies, postillion-driven, were put to this vehicle, the near leader and wheeler being ridden by postillions who led the offside ponies.

These two Royal carriages were the forerunners of many Phaetons which were later built as suitable for ladies to drive. The body design and low step were convenient for crinoline-clad ladies and the shape set their clothes off to perfection. The curving splashboards, too, offered protection from mud to the voluminous skirts, whilst the high dashboard, curved over the horses' quarters, obliterating them from view, sparing the Whip and passenger any embarrassment! Phaetons of this type were built in horse size as well as pony size and with many minor variations. A few rejected the elegant curves and replaced them with an angular body and a rein rail was put above the dashboard of some. A number were assembled without a folding hood and many had a rumble seat (Fig. 45). Those without were often turned out with two mounted grooms, called outriders, who rode behind the vehicle, the bridles on their horses matching those of the horses being driven.

As more of these Phaetons were built they became known as George IV Phaetons, Ladies Phaetons, Park Phaetons and Peters' Phaetons (after the coachbuilder who built them).

The ladies who drove these fashionable vehicles frequently carried a whip with a parasol attached to the stick. This was purely a decoration and the whip was never used for its proper purpose.

The pair of well-bred horses put to a Park Phaeton had to be outstanding in looks and way of going. It was essential that they be full of courage in order to be showy enough for Park (Hyde Park) driving, and at the same time have perfect manners and not pull. The Park Phaeton was turned out to perfection with no expense spared for Park driving on a summer's day, and it was an expensive vehicle to maintain to the required standards.

The Mail Phaeton became fashionable in 1830 and was the chief of a Phaeton tribe from which numerous other Phaetons emerged. It gained the name because its features resembled the Mail Coach. The Mail Phaeton was constructed on a similar perch and platform springs (also known as telegraph springs) (Fig. 39), giving the same quarter lock. The wheels had mail axle boxes; that is, they were secured by means of three bolts through the hub. It was a heavy and solid vehicle, exuding an aura of dignity when a handsome pair of 16 h.h. coach horses were driven from the fairly high box seat by their gentleman owner. In accordance with its coaching association, it was turned out with a road-coach flavour. The pole frequently had the steel hook at its head to carry the bars so that a team could be put to if required and steel pole chains were used.

The Mail Phaeton was favoured for both town and park driving and horsed accordingly. It was also used for country outings and posting, when lighter, faster horses might be put to. It was ideal for long journeys due to its capacity for carrying large quantities of luggage.

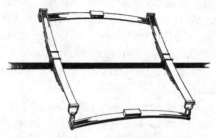

Fig. 39 Platform springing – also known as telegraph springs

Some Mail Phaetons were built so that the rear seat and the more comfortable hooded driving seat could be changed round. This arrangement enabled the vehicle to be driven by a groom, allowing the owner to rest.

A small number had a third seat to accommodate two more people, thus making the vehicle a six-seater and giving the appearance of a small char-a-banc. These were known as Beaufort Phaetons, Hunting Phaetons or Shooting Brakes.

The paint on the body of the Mail Phaeton was usually of a dark colour. The wheels were sometimes red or yellow and usually left unlined. Lining out would have been considered too feminine for such a vehicle.

The horses wore black road-coach harness with brass furniture and brown or straw collars were frequently used. It was quite usual to use the wheeler's harness of a team for a pair to a Mail Phaeton.

The Demi Mail or Semi Mail Phaeton, the Stanhope Phaeton and the T Cart Phaeton were developed from the Mail Phaeton, and were all gentlemen's carriages.

The Demi Mail or Semi Mail Phaeton differed from the Mail Phaeton in that it had no perch. A vehicle built on a perch was more difficult for a horse to pull than one built without a perch. If a wheel of a perched vehicle hit a stone, the jar was immediately felt by the horses. With a carriage without a perch the worst of the shock was taken by the springs, saving the horses from a jolt. Unperched vehicles were usually lighter and could be turned more easily, which is probably why more carriages were built without perches than with them.

The Demi Mail Phaeton was hung on elliptic springs in front, instead of platform springs, and had platform or elliptic springing behind. Frequently the Mail axles of the Mail Phaeton were rejected by the coach builders and replaced by Collinge's axles. Some Demi Mail Phaetons had an arch in the front end of the body permitting the front wheels to turn further, affording a better lock than the Mail Phaeton. The vehicle was somewhat lighter than its predecessor.

The Stanhope Phaeton was lighter again than the Demi Mail Phaeton and could be used with a single horse if desired. It was developed from a Stanhope Gig body in front and had seating for two at the rear. The original was built for the Hon. Fitzroy Stanhope by Tilbury. The Stanhope Phaeton was mounted on four elliptic springs and had an arch in the body under which the front wheels turned.

The T cart Phaeton appeared in about 1878 and was highly favoured by army officers. It was similar in shape to the Stanhope Phaeton, but smaller and lighter. As it was suitable for a single horse the rear seat accommodated only one person. This gave a bird's eye view of a T-shaped vehicle, whence it got its name.

Possibly the most fashionable town carriage in 1880 was the Spider Phaeton. This was developed by supporting a Tilbury Gig body and small rumble seat on iron branches and suspending the whole over four elliptic springs. It was a suitable vehicle for driving an exceptionally good-looking and well-bred pair. Its lightness allowed the horses complete freedom of action as it required little pulling.

A number of other Phaetons emerged during the period, made to specification and named after their owners or designers. It was this practice which makes present-day naming of individual vehicles so troublesome.

The Curricle, which was unusual in being a two-wheeled pair-horse vehicle (see page 47, Chapter 3), is thought to owe its origin to the Italians. Springs were added by the French and the English altered the body shape, introducing gracefully curving lines. The resulting vehicle was highly favoured in the early 1800s, gradually replacing the Highflyer as the fashionable carriage for gentlemen Whips. Curricles were used for long-distance journeys as well as park and town driving throughout the nineteenth century.

The hooded body accommodated the owner and a passenger and it was hung on cee springs behind. Frequently a seat for the groom was provided between the springs. A high dashboard, again, curved towards the horse's quarters.

A Curricle demanded a superb pair of perfectly matched, great-going horses, and it was an expensive though luxurious carriage to keep.

Not all Curricles were as tasteful as those driven by such personalities as the Duke of Wellington, the Marquis of Anglesey, Count d'Orsay and Charles Dickens. An extreme example of bad taste was the Curricle reputed to have been built for the actor 'Romeo' Coates. The vehicle was made of polished copper, plentifully decorated with shells. Both the carriage and the harness were emblazoned with the owner's crest, which was a crowing cock, together with the motto 'While I live, I'll crow'.

The Cabriolet (Fig. 40) was imported from France in the

Fig. 40 Cabriolet

early 1800s. Within a few years a vastly improved version succeeded the Curricle as the fashionable vehicle for gentlemen Whips to drive. It was the Count d'Orsay who was largely responsible for the improvements and refinements which developed the Cabriolet into a carriage considered suitable for 'the man about town'. It was a hooded, two-wheeled vehicle hung on cee springs, the elegantly curved body accommodating the Whip and his passenger. A rigid leather apron, fastened across the legs of the occupants, gave protection from the elements, whilst the folding hood, which was usually kept half-struck (half-shut), protected them from rain, sun and prying eyes. The shafts were curved, enabling a large horse to be put to without the vehicle having to be built especially high to accommodate him.

The stylish Cabriolet had to be turned out to perfection and a diminutive groom, called a tiger, was an essential part of the equipage. Whilst the vehicle was in motion he stood on a padded platform at the rear between the cee springs, holding on by means of two straps. When the vehicle stopped it was the tiger's job to stand in front of the horse's head. He was dressed in his owner's livery, white buckskin breeches, silk hat, mahogany-topped boots and striped yellow waistcoat from which he got his name. For a fashionable Cabriolet the tiger had to be very small, probably to create a greater contrast and make the handsome animal between the shafts look even grander.

A Cabriolet horse was outstanding in every way. He had to be well bred, as well as large, with perfect manners and faultless conformation. It was important that he should go with a flourish, but not pull. A bell used to be hung on his collar, presumably to warn other road-users at night of the approach of a fast-trotting horse. Turning out a Cabriolet in slap-up style was undoubtedly an expensive business.

The Cocking Cart, favoured in the late 1700s and early 1800s, was essentially a sporting vehicle. Its high body, which hung on side springs (Fig. 41) over two large wheels, was

Fig. 41 Side spring – also known as horizontal spring, half-elliptic spring or grasshopper spring

similar to the front boot and box seat of a coach and there was frequently a seat for a groom behind. The straight shafts ran either outside or under the body.

A Cocking Cart was usually drawn by a tandem. The boot had louvre slats on each side for ventilation for the fighting cocks which travelled in the vehicle to a Main (a match between fighting cocks).

The extensive family of Gigs possibly owe their origin to an early unsprung conveyance known as a Sedan Cart. This was a Sedan Chair on wheels with lengthened front handles to form shafts. The rear ends of these were fixed to the axle and the driver rode the horse with his legs outside the shafts.

In the middle of the eighteenth century a clumsy type of Gig was built. Its body was slightly sprung by being hung on leather straps which were fixed to iron braces rising from the rear ends of the shafts, and the wheels were small and heavy.

All Gigs had two wheels and, with a few exceptions, all had a forward-facing seat to accommodate the driver and a passenger.

One of these exceptions was the Doctor's Gig which was built with a single seat. Another was the Sulky built at the end of the eighteenth century for trotting matches. It had high wheels, straight shafts and a high single seat which was supported by a light metal frame. The modern pneumatic-tyred Sulky now used for trotting races was developed from this early Sulky.

The Suicide Gig was really a high tandem cart. It was so named because the groom's seat was built 3 feet above and behind the already high driving seat.

Many of the early Gigs produced by village coachbuilders were crude, unsprung vehicles. The seat was frequently made from a board above a pair of shafts or, at the best, a piece of wood suspended with leather from a frame. Such vehicles were cheap to produce and were often used by farmers. If they were sold for under £12, and had the words 'Taxed Cart' painted on them, they were only liable to a yearly road tax of 12s. Other two-wheeled vehicles of the period (1790) were taxed for the fee of £3 17s.

The Rib Chair Gig was an example of these early unsprung

Gigs. Round the edge of its semi-circular wooden seat were a number of perpendicular wooden spindles. Above these ribs was a curving rail forming a back seat. The body shape of the Rib Chair Gig was later adopted for a number of vehicles, including the Stanhope and Tilbury Gigs.

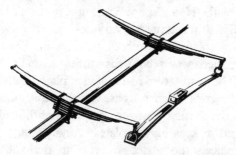

Fig. 42 Dennett springs, made up from two side springs and one cross spring

The Chair Back Gig was favoured in 1790. It consisted of a body resembling a Cabriolet which was hung by means of leather braces or elbow springs in front, and cee or whip springs behind.

The Whisky was a light vehicle also popular at this time. The chair-shaped cane body was attached to the shafts above horizontal springs. It was so named because it could *whisk* along the road at a high speed. The Whisky was thought to be the forerunner of the Dennett Gig, which was a more sophisticated version. The Dennett was originally built by a London man named Bennett. Somehow, the B became a D. One theory is that the triple-sprung (Fig. 42) vehicle was called after the three famous stage dancers of the period named the Misses Dennett.

From their humble beginning, Gigs gradually gained popularity. They were eventually being built by all the finest London craftsmen. They came in a variety of designs and methods of springing and were usually named after their coachbuilder, designer or by body characteristics.

The two most fashionable Gigs of the early 1800s were the Stanhope Gig and the Tilbury Gig. Both original vehicles were built by Tilbury of London. The Stanhope Gig, designed by the Hon. Fitzroy Stanhope, influenced a number of later Gigs. It was hung on two side- and two cross-springs, making it a comfortable vehicle to drive in. Under the rib chair seat there was a boot for storing a small amount of luggage. The shafts were made of ash, plated with iron, and fixed to the axles by span irons. Considerable vibration was caused to the shafts by a trotting horse and difficulties were experienced in keeping the plates sound. Later, lancewood shafts replaced the plated ones. The draught was also improved by using a swingle tree attached by chains to the axle, and in time rubber tyres succeeded the iron ones.

The Tilbury Gig had a similar body to the Stanhope, but no boot. It had seven springs and a quantity of ironwork. The lack of boot gave the erroneous impression that the Tilbury was a lighter vehicle than the Stanhope, although, in fact, it was, apart from the Cabriolet, the heaviest two-wheeled vehicle of that period.

By 1830 the most common vehicles to be seen on the roads were the varieties of Stanhope Gigs, and they were much favoured by bagmen (now known as commercial travellers) because there was room in the boot for carrying samples. They were light vehicles for one horse and easily driven, and for these reasons, as well as for their general convenience, they were much used by commuters, such as bankers and merchants, travelling from the suburbs to their London offices. Most suburban residences in those days were built with a small gig house as a matter of course, much as suburban houses now have their garages.

Undergraduates of Cambridge and Oxford also delighted in Gigs and used them for both tandem and single-horse driving.

The variety of Gigs available was large. There was the Liverpool Gig and the Lawton, both favoured for their elegant well-sprung bodies; the Skeleton Gig (Fig. 43), built

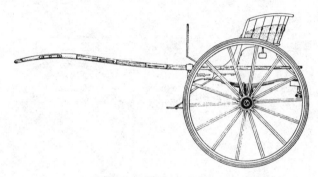

Fig. 43 Skeleton gig

with no boot and a skeleton frame; the Well Bottom Gig, with a deep well for the driver's feet; the Round Backed Gig with its rounded back rest and the Bucket Seated Gig, which had two bucket-shaped seats.

By curving the shafts in an upwards arc at the tug-stop area a gig could be built of moderate height and yet accommodate a large horse.

When a hood was added to a Gig the vehicle became known as a Hooded Gig or Buggy. If the vehicle was built on curved lines it was usually called a Buggy, and a Hooded Gig if it was a squarer carriage.

A number of American vehicles are referred to as Buggies but these are frequently four-wheelers and do not necessarily have hoods.

Dog Carts (Fig. 44) originated from Gigs at the beginning

of the nineteenth century. They were built, as their name implies, for the purpose of carrying gun dogs on shooting expeditions. The Dog Cart seated four people back to back, the driver and one passenger faced the horse and the two others sat with their backs to the front occupants. Their feet rested on a tail-board which let down on chains and the dogs

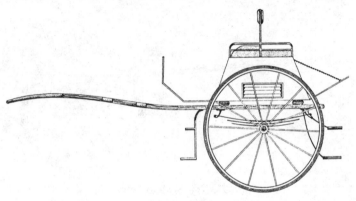

Fig. 44 Dog cart

travelled under the seats. There were venetian-type slats fitted on each side of the vehicle so that the dogs could get a plentiful supply of air.

Many varieties of Dog Cart were built. Some were given a square-shaped body profile, others were made to look more sporting by sloping the side panels inwards from the bottom to the top, giving an almost triangular impression when viewed from the side. The early vehicles were high, permitting a good view over the hedges, but later lower Dog Carts were favoured and straight shafts succeeded curved ones.

Dog cart shafts usually ran either alongside or under the body, but methods of suspension varied. Side springs, or a combination of two side- and one cross-spring, were the most usual.

Difficulties in balancing the vehicle were frequently experienced due to the varying number of people who could be accommodated. Some vehicles could be balanced by moving the whole body in relation to the axle and shafts by means of a lever. Others just had moveable seats. In both cases they were adjusted forwards when the rear seats were occupied, backwards when they were not.

Dog carts could be used for tandem driving and when this was the object the box seat was often built higher than the rear seat to facilitate control of the leader. If the shafts were replaced by a pole a pair could be put to in curricle or Cape harness.

Later on Dog Carts were built with four wheels and these could be used either with a pair or a single horse. These useful vehicles were kept on most country estates as general-purpose runabouts.

From the Dog Cart descended numerous types of Country Carts. These were used by people such as farmers, dealers and tradesmen for their daily activities. Calves, pigs and chickens could be put under the seat and covered with a net to be taken to market and families could go to church, or out for a Sunday afternoon drive, in the same vehicle.

Some Country Carts (varieties of which were also known as Village Carts and Rustic Carts) were made of oak and mahogany and were varnished. Others were painted. Most of them were built without venetian slats and some had solid sides. Still others were made lighter by replacing the upper part of the side panels with rails. The vehicles were made lower by running the shafts through the body, which, although succeeding in its objective, gave a less comfortable ride to the passengers.

Variations of these vehicles were built throughout the country, differing slightly from one county to another and were often named after their county of origin – such as Norfolk Carts and Essex Carts.

The Ralli Car also claimed the Dog Cart as an ancestor. The distinguishing feature here was the manner in which the side panels continued in an outward curve over the wheels to form splashboards, the curving being achieved by a steaming process. Frequently the shafts ran through the body, a method which caused considerable knee-rock. Various methods of suspension were used on the Ralli Car, side and Dennett springs being the most common. A few, however, were built using cee springs, and a Ralli Car, thus sprung, with shafts outside the body, was a pleasant vehicle to travel in

The Governess Car or Tub Cart was designed as a suitable vehicle in which the governess could take her charges out for an airing in comparative safety. The tub-shaped body was entered by a low step and door at the back which avoided toes from being run over if the pony should step forward. The door was shut by a handle which was frequently strategic-ally placed on the centre, outside of the door, and well out of the reach of short arms. There was no danger of children falling out of these vehicles nor of long skirts becoming entangled in spokes. In order to lessen the chances of over-turning, the centre of gravity was kept low by using a cranked axle, that is, one with two right-angle bends at each end. This enabled the body of the vehicle, which was hung on elliptic springs, to sit down between the wheels. The seats ran either side, faced inwards and were placed over the springs and the shafts went outside the body.

Governess Cars were built in large numbers around the early 1900s. They varied from the fine examples of London craftsmanship, with turned spindled sides and beautifully finished work, to the rough carts turned out by village builders.

On the other hand, many lovely vehicles were built by country experts and sent to London to be sold as 'London made'.

It was a common practice to have two pairs of wheels for one vehicle, a rubber-shod pair for the summer and an iron-shod pair for the winter.

The main disadvantage of the Governess Car is that it can only be driven from the sideways position of the rear right-hand corner, an arrangement that can prove troublesome with a pulling or difficult horse.

The Princess Cart was developed from the Governess Car and was first built by a Suffolk coachbuilder. It had a similar body shape, axle and suspension, but was entered from the front, where access could be obtained on either side of the dash. The awkward driving position of its parent vehicle was overcome by omitting the rear door and having a forward-facing seat across the back of the cart.

Brakes, or Breaks, were large four-wheeled vehicles designed for conveying quantities of luggage and passengers and were also frequently used for sporting purposes. They were suitable for exercising a team, unicorn (two wheelers and one leader) or a pair.

Private Coaches, also known as Private Drags, were built to enable the owner-driver to handle his team. A number of passengers could be taken to a race meeting, for instance, where the Drag acted as a portable grandstand. The Drag was built on similar lines to a Mail Coach but had a rear-facing seat and accommodated two, instead of one, over the hind boot. The door of this boot had hinges at the bottom so that it opened downwards on iron quadrants or on chains forming a small table. (The hind boot of a Road Coach hinged on the offside whilst the boot of a Mail Coach opened upwards under the guard's feet.) Inside the boot of the

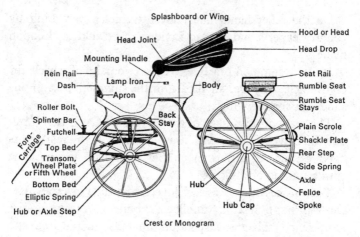

Fig. 45 Parts of a spider phaeton

Private Coach were carried tinned copper or zinc-lined –
mahogany or oak – lunch boxes. These could be pulled out
and conveniently rested on the table.

Chapter 10

CARE OF THE VEHICLE

Carriages are best housed in a building which will keep them free from excess heat, damp, ammonia fumes or direct rays of the sun. All these are harmful to the paint, leather and wood, and should be avoided. Wood is inclined to shrink in an over-warm atmosphere; cracks will appear and the paint will then split. Cushions, when not in use, can be stored in bags with camphor balls to discourage moths.

Two-wheeled vehicles should not be left with their shafts on the ground. A piece of 4 × 2 inch wood, approximately 3 feet long, wrapped in cloth, is rested with one end on the axle with the other end on the floor to the rear of the axle. The vehicle is then tipped backwards until some solid part of it (say the cross-spring of a Dennett) rests on the wood. The purpose of the cloth is to protect the paint on the vehicle from scratches. Four triangular-shaped wood blocks can be placed in front of and behind the wheels so that there is no danger of the vehicle rolling in any direction.

When the vehicle needs cleaning it must first be hosed liberally to loosen any mud or grit. Then it should be sponged, using plenty of water to prevent the varnish from getting scratched. Lastly it can be dried with a chamois leather and finished off with a soft cloth. Separate cleaning cloths should be kept for areas such as spring shackles, which may have traces of oil on them. Patent leather can be cleaned with the top of the milk or patent shoe cleaner. Metal parts should be polished. Cushions are brushed and the seat and cushion straps cleaned sparingly with saddle soap. The bolts at the end of the springs will need oiling occasionally with a thin lubricant. Any surplus oil, however, must be wiped off, otherwise it will run over painted areas, picking up grit and dust. Hooded vehicles should be left with their hoods up to prevent cracking and the leather should be wiped over occasionally with a softener. Leather cee springs and shackles also need an occasional clean with a leather preservative.

When not in use the whole vehicle should be covered with a soft, non-abrasive dust sheet. Light, waterproof covers for the body, wheels and shafts are essential if the vehicle is to be exposed to the weather during transit to a show.

A check should be made periodically to see that the wheels are running freely and that there is adequate oil or grease in the axle boxes. This entails jacking up the vehicle. First, the shafts should be supported on a trestle at their normal working height. If a gig jack is available this is put under the axle and the vehicle is easily jacked up until the wheel is well clear of the ground. Adequate clearance is important as wheels tend to lower as they come off the axle. If a gig jack is not obtainable, five-gallon oil drums and blocks of wood will serve the purpose. An oil drum is placed under the axle and wood blocks are put between the drum and the axle whilst a strong assistant lifts one side of the vehicle by the spokes of the wheel. Both wheels can be removed, leaving the vehicle safely resting with its axle on two oil drums and its shafts on the trestle. If both wheels are removed, it is advisable to mark one in some way, such as tying a piece of rag round a spoke, so that the same wheel is returned to its original axle. Sometimes, axle arms and boxes are numbered to prevent incorrect reassembly. Nuts should also be put into marked tins for their safe return to their own axle.

Varying methods are used for attaching wheels to axles. If the vehicle has a Collinge's axle, there will be a large brass or plated octagonal hub cap on which is frequently written the maker's name and town. It is attached to the hub and revolves with the wheel. A wheel spanner or large box spanner is needed to undo this. Its removal will reveal a split pin which is put through the end of the axle as a safety precaution to prevent the nuts, which are holding the wheel on, from coming off. The pin must be removed, using a pair of pliers. Next, there is an hexagonal nut on the axle which is likely to have a left-hand thread. This must be undone using a wheel or box spanner. Then there is yet another hexagonal nut to take off, a slightly larger one and with a thread opposite to the one just removed. The purpose of these opposing threads is to prevent vibration from loosening both nuts. Great care must be taken when removing and replacing the nuts so that the threads do not become damaged. The wheel is now free to slide off its axle, but it may be quite stiff because beyond the second nut will be found a metal collar known as the *collet*. Removing the wheel pulls the *collet* off as well. The purpose of the *collet* is to protect the nut from being influenced by the rotation of the wheel. The *collet* is a stiff sliding fit on the axle but it is not free to rotate because there is a flat on the inside of it which corresponds with a flat on the axle.

The removal of the wheel will reveal a leather washer. This washer is there to prevent surplus oil from pouring out over the inside of the wheel and to regulate the end play of the wheel on the axle. If the washer is found to be seriously worn it should be replaced. A saddler may be persuaded to cut a new leather washer from a piece of off-cut hide.

If the existing grease on the axle is black, hard or burnt-looking, the axle should be thoroughly cleaned with paraffin; then the axle and the channel along it can be liberally greased. Remember, however, that too thick a grease may cause the wheel to drag and that oil which is too thin will pour out.

Some vehicles of American type have one centre nut which screws on to the axle, holding the wheel on. The removal of this single central hub nut will free the wheel from its axle. When this method is used, the nuts on the left side of the vehicle undo clockwise and those on the right side undo anti-clockwise. The nuts therefore tighten in the same direction as the wheels revolve when the vehicle is going forward.

Another method is that used with a mail axle. The wheel in this case is held on by means of three bolts which run right through the hub, having three nuts at their ends. These bolts are to retain a metal collar, which remains on the axle at all times, to the inside of the wheel hub. The wheel is removed by undoing the three nuts and the wheel is then free to be drawn off its axle. Care should be taken to use the correct size spanner so that nuts and threads do not get damaged.

If the vehicle is to be kept in show condition it will probably need to be touched up and varnished every second year. Unless the carriage owner is very experienced in coach painting and has an entirely dust-free paint shop, it is probably best to take the vehicle to a craftsman for painting and varnishing.

A detailed description of carriage restoration is outside the scope of this book. Briefly, the method is as follows. All the old paint should be stripped down to the wood. Cracks and holes should be made good. A flat paint surface must be built up gradually with layers of undercoat. Each coat is applied and rubbed down until a glass-like finish is obtained. Layers of top coat are put on next, each one being slightly rubbed down. The wheels, shafts and springs are lined out. Finally, two coats of varnish complete the painting. At least nine layers of paint are necessary to give the colour the required depth. In the old days, sixteen layers of paint were frequently applied and rubbed down. Patent leather on the shafts, dash and splashboards should be renewed where applicable. If the upholstery has to be renovated it is best to use either dark colours or fawn. Bright materials are a mistake and should be avoided. Rubber matting will be needed for the floor.

INDEX

MELVIN POWERS SELF-IMPROVEMENT LIBRARY

COOKERY & HERBS

GAMBLING & POKER

HEALTH

HOBBIES

HORSE PLAYERS WINNING GUIDES

___ PARENT SURVIVAL TRAINING *Marvin Silverman, Ed.D. & David Lustig, Ph.D.* 10.00
___ SEX WITHOUT GUILT *Albert Ellis, Ph.D.* 7.00
___ SEXUALLY ADEQUATE MALE *Frank S. Caprio, M.D.* 3.00
___ SEXUALLY FULFILLED MAN *Dr. Rachel Copelan* 5.00
___ STAYING IN LOVE *Dr. Norton F. Kristy* 7.00

MELVIN POWERS' MAIL ORDER LIBRARY

___ HOW TO GET RICH IN MAIL ORDER *Melvin Powers* 20.00
___ HOW TO SELF-PUBLISH YOUR BOOK & MAKE IT A BEST SELLER *Melvin Powers* .. 20.00
___ HOW TO WRITE A GOOD ADVERTISEMENT *Victor O. Schwab* 20.00
___ MAIL ORDER MADE EASY *J. Frank Brumbaugh* 20.00

METAPHYSICS & OCCULT

___ CONCENTRATION—A GUIDE TO MENTAL MASTERY *Mouni Sadhu* 7.00
___ EXTRA-TERRESTRIAL INTELLIGENCE—THE FIRST ENCOUNTER 6.00
___ FORTUNE TELLING WITH CARDS *P. Foli* 5.00
___ HOW TO INTERPRET DREAMS, OMENS & FORTUNE TELLING SIGNS *Gettings* 5.00
___ HOW TO UNDERSTAND YOUR DREAMS *Geoffrey A. Dudley* 5.00
___ MAGICIAN—HIS TRAINING AND WORK *W. E. Butler* 7.00
___ MEDITATION *Mouni Sadhu* 10.00
___ MODERN NUMEROLOGY *Morris C. Goodman* 5.00
___ NUMEROLOGY—ITS FACTS AND SECRETS *Ariel Yvon Taylor* 5.00
___ NUMEROLOGY MADE EASY *W. Mykian* 5.00
___ PALMISTRY MADE EASY *Fred Gettings* 5.00
___ PALMISTRY MADE PRACTICAL *Elizabeth Daniels Squire* 7.00
___ PROPHECY IN OUR TIME *Martin Ebon* 2.50
___ SUPERSTITION—ARE YOU SUPERSTITIOUS? *Eric Maple* 2.00
___ TAROT *Mouni Sadhu* 10.00
___ TAROT OF THE BOHEMIANS *Papus* 7.00
___ WAYS TO SELF-REALIZATION *Mouni Sadhu* 7.00
___ WITCHCRAFT, MAGIC & OCCULTISM—A FASCINATING HISTORY *W. B. Crow* 10.00
___ WITCHCRAFT—THE SIXTH SENSE *Justine Glass* 7.00

RECOVERY

___ KNIGHT IN RUSTY ARMOR *Robert Fisher* 5.00
___ KNIGHT IN RUSTY ARMOR *Robert Fisher (Hard cover edition)* 10.00
___ KNIGHTS WITHOUT ARMOR *Aaron R. Kipnis, Ph.D. (Hard cover edition)* 10.00

SELF-HELP & INSPIRATIONAL

___ CHARISMA—HOW TO GET "THAT SPECIAL MAGIC" *Marcia Grad* 7.00
___ DAILY POWER FOR JOYFUL LIVING *Dr. Donald Curtis* 7.00
___ DYNAMIC THINKING *Melvin Powers* 5.00
___ GREATEST POWER IN THE UNIVERSE *U. S. Andersen* 7.00
___ GROW RICH WHILE YOU SLEEP *Ben Sweetland* 10.00
___ GROW RICH WITH YOUR MILLION DOLLAR MIND *Brian Adams* 7.00
___ GROWTH THROUGH REASON *Albert Ellis, Ph.D.* 10.00
___ GUIDE TO PERSONAL HAPPINESS *Albert Ellis, Ph.D. & Irving Becker, Ed.D.* 10.00
___ HANDWRITING ANALYSIS MADE EASY *John Marley* 10.00
___ HANDWRITING TELLS *Nadya Olyanova* 7.00
___ HOW TO ATTRACT GOOD LUCK *A.H.Z. Carr* 7.00
___ HOW TO DEVELOP A WINNING PERSONALITY *Martin Panzer* 7.00
___ HOW TO DEVELOP AN EXCEPTIONAL MEMORY *Young & Gibson* 10.00
___ HOW TO LIVE WITH A NEUROTIC *Albert Ellis, Ph.D.* 7.00
___ HOW TO OVERCOME YOUR FEARS *M. P. Leahy, M.D.* 3.00
___ HOW TO SUCCEED *Brian Adams* 7.00
___ HUMAN PROBLEMS & HOW TO SOLVE THEM *Dr. Donald Curtis* 5.00
___ I CAN *Ben Sweetland* 8.00
___ I WILL *Ben Sweetland* 10.00
___ KNIGHT IN RUSTY ARMOR *Robert Fisher* 5.00

_____ KNIGHT IN RUSTY ARMOR *Robert Fisher (Hard cover edition)* 10.00
_____ LEFT-HANDED PEOPLE *Michael Barsley* 5.00
_____ MAGIC IN YOUR MIND *U. S. Andersen* 10.00
_____ MAGIC OF THINKING SUCCESS *Dr. David J. Schwartz* 8.00
_____ MAGIC POWER OF YOUR MIND *Walter M. Germain* 7.00
_____ MENTAL POWER THROUGH SLEEP SUGGESTION *Melvin Powers* 3.00
_____ NEVER UNDERESTIMATE THE SELLING POWER OF A WOMAN *Dottie Walters* 7.00
_____ NEW GUIDE TO RATIONAL LIVING *Albert Ellis, Ph.D. & R. Harper, Ph.D.* 10.00
_____ PSYCHO-CYBERNETICS *Maxwell Maltz, M.D.* 7.00
_____ PSYCHOLOGY OF HANDWRITING *Nadya Olyanova* 7.00
_____ SALES CYBERNETICS *Brian Adams* 10.00
_____ SCIENCE OF MIND IN DAILY LIVING *Dr. Donald Curtis* 7.00
_____ SECRET OF SECRETS *U. S. Andersen* 7.00
_____ SECRET POWER OF THE PYRAMIDS *U. S. Andersen* 7.00
_____ SELF-THERAPY FOR THE STUTTERER *Malcolm Frazer* 3.00
_____ SUCCESS-CYBERNETICS *U. S. Andersen* 7.00
_____ 10 DAYS TO A GREAT NEW LIFE *William E. Edwards* 3.00
_____ THINK AND GROW RICH *Napoleon Hill* 8.00
_____ THINK LIKE A WINNER *Dr. Walter Doyle Staples* 10.00
_____ THREE MAGIC WORDS *U. S. Andersen* 10.00
_____ TREASURY OF COMFORT *Edited by Rabbi Sidney Greenberg* 10.00
_____ TREASURY OF THE ART OF LIVING *Sidney S. Greenberg* 7.00
_____ WHAT YOUR HANDWRITING REVEALS *Albert E. Hughes* 4.00
_____ WONDER WITHIN *Thomas F. Coyle, M.D.* 10.00
_____ YOUR SUBCONSCIOUS POWER *Charles M. Simmons* 7.00
_____ YOUR THOUGHTS CAN CHANGE YOUR LIFE *Dr. Donald Curtis* 7.00

SPORTS

_____ BILLIARDS—POCKET • CAROM • THREE CUSHION *Clive Cottingham, Jr.* 7.00
_____ COMPLETE GUIDE TO FISHING *Vlad Evanoff* 2.00
_____ HOW TO IMPROVE YOUR RACQUETBALL *Lubarsky, Kaufman & Scagnetti* 5.00
_____ HOW TO WIN AT POCKET BILLIARDS *Edward D. Knuchell* 10.00
_____ JOY OF WALKING *Jack Scagnetti* 3.00
_____ LEARNING & TEACHING SOCCER SKILLS *Eric Worthington* 3.00
_____ RACQUETBALL FOR WOMEN *Toni Hudson, Jack Scagnetti & Vince Rondone* 3.00
_____ SECRET OF BOWLING STRIKES *Dawson Taylor* 5.00
_____ SOCCER—THE GAME & HOW TO PLAY IT *Gary Rosenthal* 7.00
_____ STARTING SOCCER *Edward F. Dolan, Jr.* 3.00

TENNIS LOVER'S LIBRARY

_____ HOW TO BEAT BETTER TENNIS PLAYERS *Loring Fiske* 4.00
_____ PSYCH YOURSELF TO BETTER TENNIS *Dr. Walter A. Luszki* 2.00
_____ TENNIS FOR BEGINNERS *Dr. H. A. Murray* 2.00
_____ TENNIS MADE EASY *Joel Brecheen* 5.00
_____ WEEKEND TENNIS—HOW TO HAVE FUN & WIN AT THE SAME TIME *Bill Talbert* 3.00

WILSHIRE PET LIBRARY

_____ DOG TRAINING MADE EASY & FUN *John W. Kellogg* 5.00
_____ HOW TO BRING UP YOUR PET DOG *Kurt Unkelbach* 2.00
_____ HOW TO RAISE & TRAIN YOUR PUPPY *Jeff Griffen* 3.00

The books listed above can be obtained from your book dealer or directly from Melvin Powers
When ordering, please remit $2.00 postage for the first book and $1.00 for each additional book

Melvin Powers
12015 Sherman Road, No. Hollywood, California 91605